Houghton Mifflin Reading
Tennessee

D1370812

Teacher's Edition

Kindergarten

Wheels Go Around

Welcome to Kindergarten

Senior Authors J. David Cooper, John J. Pikulski

Authors David J. Chard, Gilbert G. Garcia, Claude N. Goldenberg, Phyllis C. Hunter, Marjorie Y. Lipson, Shane Templeton, Sheila W. Valencia, MaryEllen Vogt

Consultants Linda H. Butler, Linnea C. Ehri, Carla B. Ford

HOUGHTON MIFFLIN   BOSTON

TENNESSEE REVIEWERS

Maryellen Eaves, Cordova, Tennessee; **Tim Hamilton,** Metro/Nashville Public Schools, Tennessee; **Vicki Haney,** Metro/Nashville Public Schools, Tennessee; **Fran Hewston Gregory,** Metro/Nashville Public Schools, Tennessee; **Deborah L. Smith,** Metro/Nashville Public Schools, Tennessee; **Linda L. Wyatt,** Metro/Nashville Public Schools, Tennessee

LITERATURE REVIEWERS

Consultants: Dr. Adela Artola Allen, Associate Dean, Graduate College, Associate Vice President for Inter-American Relations, University of Arizona, Tucson, AZ; **Dr. Manley Begay,** Co-director of the Harvard Project on American Indian Economic Development, Director of the National Executive Education Program for Native Americans, Harvard University, John F. Kennedy School of Government, Cambridge, MA; **Dr. Nicholas Kannellos,** Director, Arte Publico Press, Director, Recovering the U.S. Hispanic Literacy Heritage Project, University of Houston, TX; **Mildred Lee,** author and former head of Library Services for Sonoma County, Santa Rosa, CA; **Dr. Barbara Moy,** Director of the Office of Communication Arts, Detroit Public Schools, MI; **Norma Naranjo,** Clark County School District, Las Vegas, NV; **Dr. Arlette Ingram Willis,** Associate Professor, Department of Curriculum and Instruction, Division of Language and Literacy, University of Illinois at Urbana-Champaign, IL

Teachers: Helen Brooks, Vestavia Hills Elementary School, Birmingham, Alabama; **Patricia Buchanan,** Thurgood Marshall School, Newark, Delaware; **Gail Connor,** Language Arts Resource Teacher, Duval County, Jacksonville, Florida; **Vicki DeMott,** McLean Science/Technology School, Wichita, Kansas; **Marge Egenhoffer,** Dixon Elementary School, Brookline, Wisconsin; **Mary Jew Mori,** Griffin Avenue Elementary, Los Angeles, California

PROGRAM REVIEWERS

Linda Bayer, Jonesboro, GA; **Sheri Blair,** Warner Robins, GA; **Faye Blake,** Jacksonville, FL; **Suzi Boyett,** Sarasota, FL; **Carol Brockhouse,** Madison Schools, Wayne Westland Schools, MI; **Patti Brustad,** Sarasota, FL; **Jan Buckelew,** Venice, FL; **Maureen Carlton,** Barstow, CA; **Karen Cedar,** Gold River, CA; **Karen Ciraulo,** Folsom, CA; **Marcia M. Clark,** Griffin, GA; **Kim S. Coady,** Covington, GA; **Eva Jean Conway,** Valley View School District, IL; **Marilyn Crownover,** Tustin, CA; **Carol Daley,** Sioux Falls, SD; **Jennifer Davison,** West Palm Beach, FL; **Lynne M. DiNardo,** Covington, GA; **Kathy Dover,** Lake City, GA; **Cheryl Dultz,** Citrus Heights, CA; **Debbie Friedman,** Fort Lauderdale, FL; **Anne Gaitor,** Lakeland, GA; **Rebecca S. Gillette,** Saint Marys, GA; **Buffy C. Gray,** Peachtree City, GA; **Merry Guest,** Homestead, FL; **Jo Nan Holbrook,** Lakeland, GA; **Beth Holguin,** San Jose, CA; **Coleen Howard-Whals,** St. Petersburg, FL; **Beverly Hurst,** Jacksonville, FL; **Debra Jackson,** St. Petersburg, FL; **Vickie Jordan,** Centerville, GA; **Cheryl Kellogg,** Panama City, FL; **Karen Landers,** Talladega County, AL; **Barb LeFerrier,** Port Orchard, WA; **Sandi Maness,** Modesto, CA; **Ileana Masud,** Miami, FL; **David Miller,** Cooper City, FL; **Muriel Miller,** Simi Valley, CA; **Walsetta W. Miller,** Macon, GA; **Jean Nielson,** Simi Valley, CA; **Sue Patton,** Brea, CA; **Debbie Peale,** Miami, FL; **Loretta Piggee,** Gary, IN; **Jennifer Rader,** Huntington, CA; **April Raiford,** Columbus, GA; **Cheryl Remash,** Manchester, NH; **Francis Rivera,** Orlando, FL; **Marina Rodriguez,** Hialeah, FL; **Marilynn Rose,** MI; **Kathy Scholtz,** Amesbury, MA; **Kimberly Moulton Schorr,** Columbus, GA; **Linda Schrum,** Orlando, FL; **Sharon Searcy,** Mandarin, FL; **Melba Sims,** Orlando, FL; **Judy Smith,** Titusville, FL; **Bea Tamo,** Huntington, CA; **Dottie Thompson,** Jefferson County, AL; **Dana Vassar,** Winston-Salem, NC; **Beverly Wakefield,** Tarpon Springs, FL; **Joy Walls,** Winston-Salem, NC; **Elaine Warwick,** Williamson County, TN; **Audrey N. Watkins,** Atlanta, GA; **Marti Watson,** Sarasota, FL

Supervisors: Judy Artz, Butler County, OH; **James Bennett,** Elkhart, IN; **Kay Buckner-Seal,** Wayne County, MI; **Charlotte Carr,** Seattle, WA; **Sister Marion Christi,** Archdiocese of Philadelphia, PA; **Alvina Crouse,** Denver, CO; **Peggy DeLapp,** Minneapolis, MN; **Carol Erlandson,** Wayne Township Schools, IN; **Brenda Feeney,** North Kansas City School District, MO; **Winnie Huebsch,** Sheboygan, WI; **Brenda Mickey,** Winston-Salem, NC; **Audrey Miller,** Camden, NJ; **JoAnne Piccolo,** Westminster, CO; **Sarah Rentz,** Baton Rouge, LA; **Kathy Sullivan,** Omaha, NE; **Rosie Washington,** Gary, IN; **Theresa Wishart,** Knox County Public Schools, TN

English Language Learners Reviewers: Maria Arevalos, Pomona, CA; **Lucy Blood,** NV; **Manuel Brenes,** Kalamazoo, MI; **Delight Diehn,** AZ; **Susan Dunlap,** Richmond, CA; **Tim Fornier,** Grand Rapids, MI; **Connie Jimenez,** Los Angeles, CA; **Diane Bonilla Lether,** Pasadena, CA; **Anna Lugo,** Chicago, IL; **Marcos Martel,** Hayward, CA; **Carolyn Mason,** Yakima, WA; **Jackie Pinson,** Moorpark, CA; **Jenaro Rivas,** NJ; **Jerilyn Smith,** Salinas, CA; **Noemi Velazquez,** Jersey City, NJ; **JoAnna Veloz,** NJ; **Dr. Santiago Veve,** Las Vegas, NV

Printed in the U.S.A.

ISBN-13: 978-0-618-78416-5
ISBN-10: 0-618-78416-0

1 2 3 4 5 6 7 8 9 10 B 12 11 10 09 08 07 06

CREDITS

Cover
Cover Illustration by Dave Clegg.

Photography
Theme Opener © Preston Lyon/Index Stock Imagery.

Assignment Photography
T23, T43, T49 © HMCo./Parker/Boon/Productions. All other photography © HMCo./Joel Benjamin.

Illustration
Theme Class Project art by Tim Johnson.
All other child art by Morgan-Cain & Associates.

ACKNOWLEDGMENTS

Grateful acknowledgment is made for permission to reprint copyrighted material as follows:

Theme 7

Mr. Gumpy's Motor Car, by John Burningham. Copyright © 1973 by John Burningham. Used by permission of HarperCollins Publishers.

The Little Engine That Could™, (Original Classic Edition) by Watty Piper, illustrated by George and Doris Hauman. Copyright © 1976, 1961, 1954, 1945, 1930 by Platt & Munk Publishers, a division of Grosset & Dunlap Inc., which is a division of Penguin Putnam Inc. Reprinted by permission of Grosset & Dunlap Inc., a division of Penguin Putnam Inc. All rights reserved. From *The Pony Engine,* by Mabel C. Bragg, copyright by George H. Doran & Co. *The Little Engine That Could,* engine design, and "I Think I Can" are trademarks of Platt & Munk. Platt & Munk is a trademark of Grosset & Dunlap, Inc., Reg. U. S. Pat. & Tm Off. Published by arrangement with Grosset & Dunlap, Inc., a member of Penguin Putnam Books for Young Readers, a division of Penguin Putnam Inc.

The Wheels on the Bus, by Maryann Kovalski. Copyright © 1987 by Maryann Kovalski. Reprinted by arrangement with Kids Can Press Ltd. (Toronto, Canada) and Little, Brown and Company (New York).

Vroom, Chugga, Vroom-Vroom, by Anne Miranda, illustrated by David Murphy. Text copyright © 1998 by Anne Miranda. Illustrations copyright © 1998 by David Murphy. Reprinted by permission of Turtle Books.

Wheels Go Around

OBJECTIVES

Phonemic Awareness blending phonemes; segmenting phonemes

Phonics sounds for *D, d; Z, z;* words with short *i*

High-Frequency Words *for, have*

Reading Strategies summarize; monitor/clarify; question; phonics/decoding

Comprehension Skills text organization and summarizing; cause and effect; making predictions

Vocabulary opposites; position words; parts of a car; words for travel

Fluency build reading fluency

Concepts of Print first-last letter; matching words; capital letters; spoken word to print

Writing signs; journals; class story; report

Listening/Speaking/Viewing supports vocabulary and writing

Wheels Go Around

C O N T E N T S

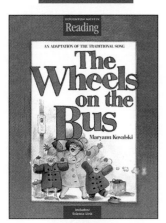

Week 1

Skill Lessons. See Daily Lesson Plans.

Books for Small-Group Reading

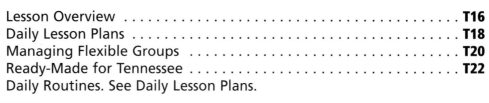

Big Book

Nonfiction

Decodable
Text

On My Way
Practice Reader
Below Level/On Level
(Week 3)

Leveled Reader
On Level

Little Big Book
On Level/Above Level

Decodable
Text

On My Way
Practice Reader
Below Level/On Level (Week 3)

Leveled Reader
On Level

Little Big Book
On Level/Above Level

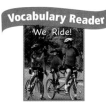

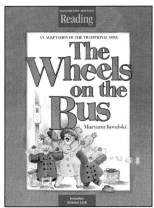

Nonfiction

Decodable
Text

On My Way
Practice Reader
Below Level/On Level

Leveled Reader
On Level

Little Big Books
On Level/Above Level

Bibliography

BOOKS FOR SMALL-GROUP READING, READ ALOUD, AND FLUENCY BUILDING

 To build oral language, vocabulary and fluency, choose books from this list for additional read aloud opportunities and small-group reading.

Key

 Science

 Social Studies

 Multicultural

 Music

 Math

 Classic

 Art

 Career

Classroom Bookshelf

BOOKS FOR BROWSING

My Car
by Byron Barton
Greenwillow 2001 (24p)
A driver introduces the features of his car in this bold, brightly illustrated story.

Dump Trucks
by Judith Jango-Cohen
Lerner 2003 (32p) also paper
Photos and brief text show dump trucks doing many jobs. See others in series.

Emergency!
by Margaret Mayo
Carolrhoda 2002 (32p)
Fire engines, ambulances, police cars, and tow trucks race to the rescue in this action-filled book.

Get to Work, Trucks!
by Don Carter
Roaring Brook 2002 (24p)
Eight hardworking machines do all kinds of jobs at a construction site.

ABC Drive! *
by Naomi Howland
Clarion 2000 (32p)
A boy on a car trip sees things related to vehicles for every letter of the alphabet.

So Many Circles, So Many Squares
by Tana Hoban
Greenwillow 1998 (32p)
The geometric concepts of circles and squares are presented in photos of wheels, signs, and other objects.

Delivery
by Anastasia Suen
Viking 1999 (32p)
Trucks, bicycles, taxis, and other vehicles deliver everything from newspapers to groceries.

Circular Movement
by Lola M. Schaefer
Pebble 2000 (24p)
Photographs and simple text describe objects that move in circles.

Traffic Jam
by Seymour Chwast
Houghton 1999 (32p)
In a book with foldout pages, a cat and her kitten cause a traffic jam when they cross the road.

Night at the Fair
by Donald Crews
Greenwillow 1998 (32p)
Nighttime is a great time to be at the fair, and the best ride of all is the giant Ferris wheel.

My Puffer Train
by Mary Murphy
Houghton 1999 (32p)
On the way to the seashore in his train, Penguin invites other animals aboard.

BOOKS FOR TEACHER READ ALOUD

One Wheel Wobbles
by Carole Lexa Schaefer
Candlewick 2003 (32p)
A motorcycle-riding, trike-peddling, truck-driving, roller-skating family sets off in a parade.

Rattletrap Car
by Phyllis Root
Candlewick 2001 (32p)
A family improvises clever solutions when their old jalopy breaks down during a trip.

The Bus for Us
by Suzanne Bloom
Boyds Mills 2001 (32p)
As fire trucks, taxis, and garbage trucks go by, a girl wonders where the school bus is.

Racer Dogs
by Bob Kolar
Dutton 2003 (32p)
Bingo, Dodger, Zigzag and other dogs all want to win the big race in this funny, rhyming story.

Double Those Wheels
by Nancy Raines Day
Dutton 2003 (32p)
Monkey makes a special delivery with a little help from a lot of wheels.

Mike Mulligan and His Steam Shovel
by Virginia Lee Burton
Houghton 1939 (48p) also paper
*Mike and his steam shovel, Mary Anne, don't give up when they lose their job. **Available in Spanish as** Mike Mulligan y su máquina maravillosa.*

Curious George Rides a Bike *
by H. A. Rey
Houghton 1952 (48p) also paper
Curious George helps a boy with his paper route and gets into all sorts of trouble.

Duck in the Truck
by Jez Alborough
Harper 2000 (32p)
A frog, a goat, and a sheep help Duck when his truck gets stuck.

*Included in Classroom Bookshelf, Level K

On the Move

by Henry Pluckrose
Watts 1998 (32p) also paper
Photos and text present all kinds of vehicles that help people get from place to place.

Truck Talk
by Bobbi Katz
Cartwheel 1997 (32p)
In poems paired with photos, trucks talk about what they do.

Window Music
by Anastasia Suen
Viking 1998 (32p)

A train clickety clacks its way over hills and through valleys.

The Little Engine That Could

by Watty Piper
Putnam 1930 (48p) also paper
A small but determined train engine helps get food and toys to children waiting in a valley. **Available in Spanish as** La pequeña locomotora que sí pudo.

Seymour Simon's Book of Trucks

by Seymour Simon
Harper 2000 (32p)
Photographs of trucks accompany descriptions of the jobs they do.

Seals on the Bus
by Lenny Hort
Holt 2000 (32p)
At every stop, animals join a family riding a bus in this popular song.

Sheep in a Jeep*
by Nancy Shaw
Houghton 1986 (32p)

Five sheep out for a ride in their Jeep run into trouble.

Five Little Monkeys Wash the Car
by Eileen Christelow
Clarion 2000 (32p)

Five monkeys try to persuade their crocodile neighbors to buy their old car. See others in series.

BOOKS FOR PHONICS READ ALOUD

Vroomaloom Zoom

by John Coy
Crown 2000 (32p)
Carmela and her dad go for a ride in their big yellow car in this rhyming story.

Dazzling Diggers
by Tony Mitton
Kingfisher 1997 (24p)
Animals operate digging machines that move rubble and do other things in this rhyming story.

Mama Zooms
by Jane Cowen-Fletcher
Scholastic 1993 (32p) also paper

A boy pretends his mama's wheelchair is everything from a racehorse to a spaceship.

Technology

Computer Software Resources

- **Lexia Quick Phonics Assessment CD-ROM**
- **Lexia Phonics Intervention CD-ROM: Primary**
- **Published by Sunburst Technology***
  Tenth Planet™ Vowels: Short and Long
  Curious George® Pre-K ABCs
  First Phonics
- **Published by The Learning Company**
  Dr. Seuss's ABC™
  Paint, Write, & Play!™
  ¡Vamos a Jugar, Pintar, y Escribir!

Video Cassettes

- **The Alphabet Train.** *Big Kids*
- **Mike Mulligan and His Steam Shovel** *by Virginia Lee Burton. Weston Woods*
- **Cars! Cars! Cars!** *Big Kids*
- **The Little Engine That Could** *by Watty Piper. Weston Woods*
- **I Dig Dirt.** *Big Kids*
- **Curious George Rides a Bike** *by H. A. Rey. Weston Woods*
- **Big Work Trucks.** *Big Kids*
- **Fire Trucks in Action.** *Big Kids*

Audio

- **Sheep in a Jeep** *by Margot Apple. Houghton*
- **Truck Song** *by Diane Siebert. Live Oak*
- **The Bear's Bicycle** *by Emilie Warren McLeod. Live Oak*
- **Choo Choo** *by Virginia Lee Burton. Houghton*
- **CD-ROM for** *Wheels Go Around*. *Houghton Mifflin Company*
  * *©Sunburst Technology. All Rights Reserved.*

Technology Resources addresses are on page R16.

Education Place

www.eduplace.com *Log on to Education Place for more activities relating to Wheels Go Around.*

Book Adventure

www.bookadventure.org *This Internet reading-incentive program provides thousands of titles for children to read.*

Theme Skills Overview

Teacher Read Aloud
Wheels Around
Nonfiction

Big Book
The Wheels on the Bus
Fiction

Pacing
Approximately 3 weeks

Combination Classrooms

See the **Combination Classroom Planning Guide** for lesson planning and management support.

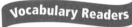

Nonfiction

Leveled Readers

Half-Day Kindergarten

Focus on lessons for tested skills marked with **T**. Then choose other activities as time allows.

Learning to Read

Phonemic Awareness

Phonics

High-Frequency Words

Comprehension

Concepts of Print

- Blending Phonemes **T**
- Segmenting Phonemes **T**
- Beginning Sound /d/
- Initial Consonant *d* **T**
- Blending Short *i* Words **T**
- Concepts of Print **T**
- High-Frequency Word: *for* **T**

Guiding Comprehension
- Text Organization and Summarizing **T**
- Comprehension Strategy: Summarize
- Decodable Text

"Big Rig"

Science Link *Look for Wheels*
Nonfiction

Books for Small-Group Reading
- Fluency Practice
- Independent Reading

Take-Home Phonics Library

Vocabulary Reader

Leveled Reader

Little Big Book

Word Work

High-Frequency Word Practice

Building Words

High-Frequency Words: *a, and, for, go, here, I, is, like, my, see, to*

Words with Short *i* or Short *a*

Writing and Oral Language

Vocabulary

Writing

Listening/Speaking/Viewing

Vocabulary Reader

Vocabulary: Using Opposites

Shared Writing: Writing About Signs

Interactive Writing: Writing About Signs

Independent Writing: Journals

Listening/Speaking/Viewing

T Skill tested on Emerging Literacy Survey, Integrated Theme Test and/or Weekly or Theme Skills Test

Target Skills

Phonemic Awareness
Phonics
Comprehension
Vocabulary
Fluency

Week 2	Week 3: Tested Skill Review
Teacher Read Aloud *The Little Engine That Could* Fiction **Big Books** *Vroom, Chugga, Vroom-Vroom* Fantasy 	**Teacher Read Aloud** *Mr. Gumpy's Motor Car* A Contemporary British Tale **Big Books** *The Wheels on the Bus* *Vroom, Chugga, Vroom-Vroom*
⊙ **Blending Phonemes** T ⊙ **Segmenting Phonemes** T ⊙ **Beginning Sound** /z/ ⊙ **Initial Consonant** *z* T ⊙ **Blending Short *i* Words** T ⊙ **Concepts of Print** T ⊙ **High-Frequency Word:** *have* T **Guiding Comprehension** ⊙ **Cause and Effect** T ⊙ **Comprehension Strategy: Monitor/Clarify** ⊙ **Decodable Text** "Tan Van" **Science Link** *Cool Wheels!* Nonfiction	⊙ **Blending Phonemes** T ⊙ **Segmenting Phonemes** T ⊙ **Beginning Sounds** /k/ and /z/ ⊙ **Initial Consonants** *d* and *z* T ⊙ **Blending Short *i* Words** T ⊙ **Concepts of Print** T ⊙ **High-Frequency Words:** *for, have* T **Guiding Comprehension** ⊙ **Making Predictions** T ⊙ **Comprehension Strategy: Summarize; Question** ⊙ **Decodable Text** "Zig Pig and Dan Cat" **Revisit the Links** *Look for Wheels* and *Cool Wheels!*
Take-Home Phonics Library **Vocabulary Reader** **Leveled Reader** **Little Big Book**	⊙ **On My Way Practice Reader** **Take-Home Phonics Library** **Vocabulary Reader** **Leveled Reader** **Little Big Book**
High-Frequency Words: *I, see, my, like, a, to, and, go, for, have* **Words with Short *i* or Short *a***	**High-Frequency Words:** *I, see, my, like, a, to, and, go, for, have* **Words with Short *i* or Short *a***
Vocabulary Reader ⊙ **Vocabulary: Using Position Words** ✎ **Shared Writing:** Writing a Class Story **Interactive Writing:** Writing a Class Story **Independent Writing:** Journals Listening/Speaking/Viewing	**Vocabulary Reader** ⊙ **Vocabulary: Using Opposites; Words for Travel** ✎ **Shared Writing:** Writing a Report **Interactive Writing:** Writing a Report **Independent Writing:** Journals Listening/Speaking/Viewing

Concepts of Print lessons teach important foundational skills for Phonics.

Cross-Curricular Activities

Week 1:
Setting Up Centers Activities
Theme Class Project

Week 2:
Setting Up Centers Activities
Theme Class Project

Week 3:
Setting Up Centers Activities
Theme Class Project

Additional Theme Resources

- Challenge/Extension Activities
- Blackline Masters
- Songs
- Word Lists

Technology

Education Place
www.eduplace.com

Log on to Education Place for more activities relating to *Wheels Go Around*.

Lesson Planner CD-ROM
Customize your planning for *Wheels Go Around* with the Lesson Planner CD-ROM.

Curious George® Learns Phonics
Contains interactive phonics activities for beginning readers.

Management Routines

Notes from an Alphafriend

Use the **Alphafriend** of the week to help you reinforce classroom rules or offer children a pat on the back.

- Before class, slip a hand-written note behind the **Alphafriend** card in the pocket chart.

- Allow the note to protrude a bit so that children will eventually discover it and bring it to you.

- The note from the "friend" can compliment children on their new skills, mention a classroom routine that could use better participation, or remind children of an upcoming event.

- If children enjoy hearing from the **Alphafriend,** you may want to make the notes a regular feature!

You do a ducky job with those blending games!

Instructional Routines

Phonics: Review Sounds

Are there children in your class who did not understand what you meant by "the sound for a letter," initially, or who have trouble remembering certain consonants? To help these children, a regular cycle of review is built into the routine for every consonant lesson, in the **Compare and Review** step. Beginning with this theme, there is a second review cycle for potentially troublesome consonants: from time to time, the main lesson now reviews selected letter sounds.

As you use the phonics reviews, focus on children who need extra support. For other children, these routines will confirm past learning and provide new practice. Are there children who use phonics confidently? Assign a writing task instead, with a topic or character whose name starts with the target sound.

Alphafriend Alert

Some children will benefit from one-on-one work with phonemic awareness or phonics skills. Give each child a stick puppet of the **Alphafriend** of the week. Children can hold up their puppets as a signal to you when they need some help figuring out a new word in a story or completing a phonics page.

Theme Class Project

Independent Activities

Have children work on this theme project at any time during the theme while you work with small groups.

Additional Independent Activities

- **Classroom Management Handbook,** pp. 146–169

- **Challenge Handbook,** pp. 48–55

- Setting Up Centers, pp. T22–T23, T78–T79, T138–T139

Look for more activities in the Classroom Management Kit.

The Wheel Museum

Materials   toy vehicles • small household objects with wheels • video and picture books about wheels . . . .

Making Theme Connections

Before beginning the project, display theme resources such as the **Theme Poster,** the **Theme Poem,** and **Big Books.** Lead a discussion about how children use wheels in daily life.

What to Do

- Display the **Theme Poster** as a background for a Wheel Museum. Add interesting objects for investigation.

- Children can bring in toy vehicles or pictures of vehicles. They can tell how each one is used and how many wheels it has. (See Photo #1.)

- Include "hands-on" displays with items such as a toy tractor, a toy train engine and an egg beater, and let children investigate how the wheels or gears work. (See Photo #2.)

- Provide picture books or a video about wheels. (See Photo #3.)

- Children who are interested in special wheels (windmills, water wheels, or paddle-wheel boats) can ask parents or the librarian to help them learn more.

- At the end of the theme, children can make "wheel" posters and report what they have learned about wheels. (See Photo #4.)

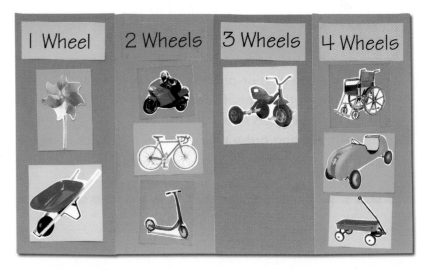

1 Children can talk about the wheels on toy vehicles or on vehicles in pictures.

2 Let children investigate how wheels or gears work at "hands-on" displays.

3 Children can enjoy picture books or videos about wheels.

4 At the end of the theme, children can make "wheel" posters and report to classmates or parents what they have learned.

REACHING ALL LEARNERS

Challenge

Put out a supply of shoeboxes, dowels, spools, pipe cleaners, and other materials, and invite small groups to build a model vehicle. They can tell about their invention and the problems they had to solve.

Planning for Assessment

During instruction in Theme 7 . . .

1 SCREENING AND DIAGNOSIS

If you have used the **Emerging Literacy Survey** to determine children's levels in phonemic awareness, letter recognition, and beginning decoding skills, you might want to readminister all or parts of the survey for continuing diagnosis.

Familiarity with Print	• Concepts of print • Letter naming
Phonemic Awareness	• Rhyme • Beginning sounds • Blending and segmenting onsets and rimes • Blending and segmenting phonemes
Beginning Reading and Writing	• Word recognition • Word writing • Sentence dictation

To determine individual children's specific instructional needs and to plan instruction, you might consider readministering one or both of the following tests:

- **Leveled Reading Passages Assessment Kit**
- **Lexia Quick Phonics Assessment CD-ROM**

2 MONITORING PROGRESS

To ensure that children are making adequate progress throughout the theme, use the following resources:

- Monitoring Student Progress boxes
- Theme 7 Observation Checklist
- Theme 7 **Theme Skills Test**
- **Emerging Literacy Survey** (See above.)
- After completing Theme 8, administer the Themes 7–8 **Integrated Theme Test**.

3 MANAGING AND REPORTING

 **Technology**   To manage your assessment information, record each child's performance on the **Learner Profile CD-ROM**.

Kindergarten Benchmarks
Documenting Adequate Yearly Progress

For your planning, listed here are the instructional goals and activities that help develop benchmark behaviors for kindergartners. Use this list to plan instruction and to monitor children's progress. See the checklist of skills found on TE page T185.

Theme Lessons and Activities	Benchmark Behaviors
Listening Comprehension/Oral Language/Vocabulary	
• rhymes, chants, motion songs • story discussions	• listen to a story attentively • participate in story discussions
Phonemic Awareness	
• blending and segmenting phonemes	• blend sounds into meaningful units
Phonics	
• initial consonants *d, z* • short *i* words	• name single letters and their sounds • decode some common CVC words
Concepts of Print	
• first/last letter of a written word; all capital letters for emphasis; matching spoken words to print; matching words	• recognize common print conventions
Reading and Fluency	
• decodable texts	• read and write a few words
Vocabulary: High-Frequency Words	
• high-frequency words *for, have*	• select a letter to represent a sound
Comprehension	
• text organization and summarizing; cause and effect; inferences: making predictions	• think critically about a text • use effective reading strategies
Writing and Language	
• writing simple phrases or sentences • journal writing	• label pictures using phonetic spellings • write independently

Launching the Theme

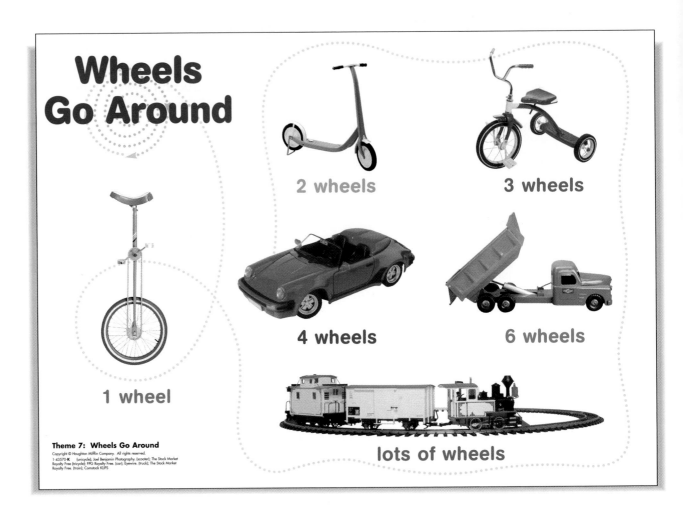

Wheels
Go Around

1 wheel

2 wheels

3 wheels

4 wheels

6 wheels

lots of wheels

Using the Theme Poster

In this theme, children will learn about all kinds of wheels. Display the **Theme Poster**, see how many of the vehicles children recognize, and compare the numbers and types of wheels.

Use the Theme Poster throughout the theme. During the theme, children can tape on captioned drawings to extend the poster's purpose.

- **Week 1:** Two good sources of information are the **Read Aloud** *Wheels Around* and the **Science Link** *Look for Wheels.* After sharing these selections, children can add drawings or magazine pictures to the poster to show unusual wheels such as a merry-go-round, a Ferris wheel, or a hamster's wheel.

- **Week 2:** The **Science Link** *Cool Wheels!* features people-powered and motor-powered vehicles. Children can rearrange the drawings on their poster into those categories or others.

- **Week 3:** The characters in *Mr. Gumpy's Motor Car* must solve the problem of wheels stuck in the mud. Children might add a new "Fixing Problems" section to their poster: changing a tire or using a bicycle pump.

Combination Classroom

See the **Combination Classroom Plannning Guide** for lesson planning and management support.

Using the Theme Poem: "Stop and Go"

Make a large cardboard traffic light. Include holes for the lights and sheets of red, yellow, and green paper attached to the back with tape hinges.

- Share the poem.
- Then have children "drive" in a circle and obey your signal as you change the lights.
- Add the traffic signal to your Dramatic Play Center.

Read aloud other poems. Poems help develop children's oral comprehension and listening skills. You may want to choose other poems to read aloud from *Higglety Pigglety: A Book of Rhymes*.

Higglety Pigglety: A Book of Rhymes, page 30

Monitoring Student Progress

Monitoring Progress

Throughout the theme, monitor your children's progress by using the following program features in the **Teacher's Edition**:

- Guiding Comprehension questions
- Literature response groups
- Skill lesson applications
- Monitoring Student Progress boxes
- Theme Wrap-Up, pages T186–T187

Classroom Management

At any time during the theme, you can assign the Theme Class Project on **Teacher Edition** pages T10–T11 while you provide differentiated instruction to small groups.

Additional independent activity centers related to specific selections can be found in the **Teacher's Edition**.

- Setting Up Centers, Week 1, pages T22–T23
- Setting Up Centers, Week 2, pages T78–T79
- Setting Up Centers, Week 3, pages T138–T139

Home Connection

Send home the theme newsletter for *Wheels Go Around* to introduce the theme and suggest home activities (See **Teacher's Resource Blackline Masters** 98 or 99.)

For other suggestions relating to *Wheels Go Around*, see **Home/Community Connections**.

Lesson Overview

Literature

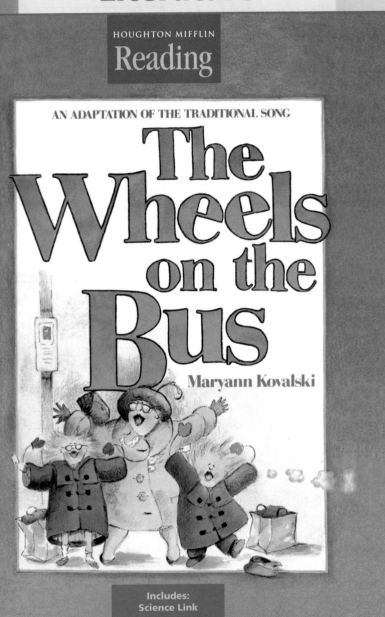

HOUGHTON MIFFLIN
Reading

AN ADAPTATION OF THE TRADITIONAL SONG

The Wheels on the Bus

Maryann Kovalski

Includes:
Science Link

Selection Summary

A grandmother and her grandchildren sing a song about a bus as they wait at a bus stop.

1 Teacher Read Aloud

• *Wheels Around*

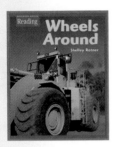

2 Big Book

• *The Wheels on the Bus*
  Genre: Fiction

3 Decodable Text

Phonics Library

• "Big Rig"

4 Science Link

This Link appears after the main Big Book selection.

Leveled Books

Vocabulary Reader

- Below Level, ELL
- Lesson

Leveled Reader

- On Level, Above Level
- Lesson
- Take-Home Version

Plus!
Online Leveled Books

Instructional Support

Planning and Practice

Tennessee Teacher's Edition

Teacher's Resources

Alphafriends

Practice book

Differentiated Instruction

Intervention/Extra Support

English Language Learners

Challenge

Ready-Made Centers

Phonics Center

Building Vocabulary

Reading in Science and Social Studies
- 30 books and activities
- support for Tennessee content standards

Hands-On Literacy Centers for Week 1
- activities
- manipulatives
- routines

Technology

Audio Selection
The Wheels on the Bus

Curious George **Learns Phonics**

www.eduplace.com
- over 1,000 Online Leveled Books

Daily Lesson Plans

Technology
Lesson Planner CD-ROM allows you to customize the chart below to develop your own lesson plans.

T Skill tested on Weekly or Theme Skills Test and/or Integrated Theme Test

 Tennessee Curriculum Standards indicated in blue.

60–90 minutes

Learning to Read

Phonemic Awareness

Phonics

High-Frequency Words

Comprehension

Concepts of Print

Vocabulary Reader
Trolley Ride

The Parade
Leveled Reader

DAY 1
 *Wheels Around*

K.1.03.a, K.1.07.d, K.1.07.e

Daily Routines, T24–T25
Calendar, Message, High-Frequency Words

Phonemic Awareness T K.1.04.b, K.1.04.c

Teacher Read Aloud, T26–T27 K.1.02

Comprehension Strategy, T26 K.1.09.b
Summarize

Comprehension Skill, T26 K.1.08.b, K.1.09
Text Organization and Summarizing **T**

Phonemic Awareness, T28–T29 K.1.05.b, K.1.05.c
Beginning Sound /d/ **T**

Cross-Curricular Activity, T23 SS.K.1.02.c

Leveled Reader
K.1.04, K.1.05, K.1.09

DAY 2
The Wheels on the Bus

K.1.01.e, K.1.01.i, K.1.07.d

Daily Routines, T32–T33
Calendar, Message, High-Frequency Words

Phonemic Awareness T
K.1.04.b, K.1.04.c

Reading the Big Book, T34–T35 K.1.06

Comprehension Strategy, T34 K.1.09.b
Summarize

Comprehension Skill, T34 K.1.08.b, K.1.09
Text Organization and Summarizing **T**

Phonics, T36–T37 K.1.05.b, K.1.05.c
Initial Consonant *d* **T**

High-Frequency Word, T38–T39
New Word: *for* **T** K.1.07.e, K.3.03

Leveled Reader
K.1.04, K.1.05, K.1.09

30–45 minutes

Word Work

High-Frequency Word Practice

Building Words

High-Frequency Word Practice, T30
Words: *a, and, go, I, see, to* K.1.07.e, K.3.03

High-Frequency Word Practice, T40
Building Sentences K.1.07.e, K.3.03, K.3.04.b

30–45 minutes

Writing and Oral Language

Vocabulary

Writing

Listening/Speaking/Viewing

Oral Language: Vocabulary, T31
Using Opposites K.1.01.d, K.1.07

Vocabulary Reader K.1.07

Vocabulary Reader K.1.07

Vocabulary Expansion, T41 K.1.07
Using Opposites

Listening/Speaking/Viewing, T41
K.1.01.f, K.1.07, K.1.11.b

 ## Half-Day Kindergarten
Focus on lessons for tested skills marked with **T**. Then choose other activities as time allows.

Tennessee English/Language Arts Curriculum Standards
and
Houghton Mifflin Reading

Grade K

For use with each Daily Lesson Plan

Grade K Learning Expectations

Reading

K.1.01 Develop oral language.
K.1.02 Develop listening skills.
K.1.03 Demonstrate knowledge of concepts of print.
K.1.04 Develop and maintain phonemic awareness.
K.1.05 Develop and use decoding strategies to read unfamiliar words.
K.1.06 Read to develop fluency, expression, accuracy, and confidence.
K.1.07 Develop and extend reading vocabulary.
K.1.08 Develop and use pre-reading strategies.
K.1.09 Use active comprehension strategies to derive meaning while reading and check for understanding after reading.
K.1.10 Introduce informational skills to facilitate learning.
K.1.11 Develop skills to facilitate reading to learn in a variety of content areas.
K.1.12 Read independently for a variety of purposes.
K.1.13 Experience various literary genres.
K.1.14 Develop and maintain a motivation to read.

Writing

K.2.01 Use a variety of pre-writing strategies.
K.2.02 Write for a variety of purposes.
K.2.03 Show evidence of drafting and revision with written work.
K.2.04 Include editing before the completion of finished work.
K.2.05 Evaluate own and others' writing.
K.2.06 Experience numerous publishing opportunities.
K.2.07 Write narrative accounts.
K.2.08 Write frequently across content areas.
K.2.09 Write expressively using original ideas, reflections, and observations.
K.2.10 Write in response to literature.
K.2.11 Write in a variety of modes and genres.

Elements of Language

K.3.01 Demonstrate knowledge of standard English usage.
K.3.02 Demonstrate knowledge of standard English mechanics.
K.3.03 Demonstrate knowledge of standard English spelling.
K.3.04 Demonstrate knowledge of correct sentence structure.

Curriculum Standards Achieved in Theme 7

Week 1: Wheels Around / The Wheels on the Bus

Daily Lesson Plans, T18–T19

I	**K.1.01.e**	Participate in group discussion
I	**K.1.01.f**	Creative responses to text
I	**K.1.01.i**	Dramatize/retell learned material
I	**K.1.02**	Develop listening skills
I	**K.1.03.a**	Identify labels/logos/signs
I	**K.1.04**	Develop phonemic awareness
I	**K.1.04.a**	Understand phoneme is distinct sound
I	**K.1.04.b**	Sound stretching to identify phoneme
I	**K.1.04.c**	Blend sound of each spoken phoneme
I	**K.1.04.g**	Know words made up of syllables
I	**K.1.05**	Develop and use decoding strategies
I	**K.1.05.b**	Written letter sequence/spoken sequence
I	**K.1.05.c**	Decode using letter-sound matches
I	**K.1.05.d**	Understand the alphabetic principle

I	**K.1.06**	Read to develop fluency
I	**K.1.07**	Develop and extend reading vocabulary
I	**K.1.07.d**	Use word families/word walls
I	**K.1.07.e**	Read some words by sight
I	**K.1.08.b**	Relate background knowledge
I	**K.1.09**	Use active comprehension strategies
I	**K.1.09.b**	Check reading understanding
I	**K.1.11.b**	Use illustrations to gather meaning
I	**K.2.07**	Write narrative accounts
I	**K.2.08.d**	Shared writing: arts/personal life
I	**K.2.09.b**	Write/draw to express opinions
I	**K.2.11.a**	Illustrate and/or write in journals
I	**K.3.03**	Demonstrate spelling of English
I	**K.3.04.b**	Logical words/appropriate word order
	SS.K.1.02.c	Transportation and environment

continues

186510

Curriculum Standards Achieved in Theme 7

Week 2: The Little Engine That Could / Vroom, Chugga, Vroom-Vroom

Daily Lesson Plans, T74–T75

- I **K.1.01.a** Expand oral language
- I **K.1.01.i** Dramatize/retell learned material
- I **K.1.02** Develop listening skills
- I **K.1.03.a** Identify labels/logos/signs
- I **K.1.03.b** Understand print has meaning
- I **K.1.04** Develop phonemic awareness
- I **K.1.04.b** Sound stretching to identify phoneme
- I **K.1.04.c** Blend sound of each spoken phoneme
- I **K.1.04.e** Recognize and produce rhyming words
- I **K.1.04.f** Words: same beginning/ending sound
- I **K.1.05** Develop and use decoding strategies
- I **K.1.05.a** Upper/lowercase letters of alphabet
- I **K.1.05.b** Written letter sequence/spoken sequence
- I **K.1.05.c** Decode using letter-sound matches
- I **K.1.05.d** Understand the alphabetic principle
- I **K.1.06** Read to develop fluency
- I **K.1.07** Develop and extend reading vocabulary
- I **K.1.07.d** Use word families/word walls
- I **K.1.07.e** Read some words by sight
- I **K.1.08.b** Relate background knowledge
- I **K.1.08.d** Use illustrations to preview text
- I **K.1.09** Use active comprehension strategies
- I **K.1.11.b** Use illustrations to gather meaning
- I **K.1.13.i** Sequence events in a story
- I **K.2.01.a** Brainstorm ideas with teacher/peers
- I **K.2.02.a** Write to acquire/exhibit knowledge
- I **K.2.07** Write narrative accounts
- I **K.2.09.b** Write/draw to express opinions
- I **K.2.11.a** Illustrate and/or write in journals
- I **K.3.03** Demonstrate spelling of English
- I **K.3.04.b** Logical words/appropriate word order
- **SS.K.1.02.c** Transportation and environment

Week 3: Mr. Gumpy's Motor Car / The Wheels on the Bus / Vroom, Chugga, Vroom-Vroom

Daily Lesson Plans, T134–T135

- I **K.1.01.e** Participate in group discussion
- I **K.1.01.f** Creative responses to text
- I **K.1.02** Develop listening skills
- I **K.1.03.f** Distinguish letters from words
- I **K.1.04** Develop phonemic awareness
- I **K.1.04.b** Sound stretching to identify phoneme
- I **K.1.04.c** Blend sound of each spoken phoneme
- I **K.1.04.f** Words: same beginning/ending sound
- I **K.1.05** Develop and use decoding strategies
- I **K.1.05.b** Written letter sequence/spoken sequence
- I **K.1.05.c** Decode using letter-sound matches
- I **K.1.05.d** Understand the alphabetic principle
- I **K.1.06** Read to develop fluency
- I **K.1.07** Develop and extend reading vocabulary
- I **K.1.07.d** Use word families/word walls
- I **K.1.07.e** Read some words by sight
- I **K.1.08** Develop/use pre-reading strategies
- I **K.1.08.c** Make predictions about text
- I **K.1.09** Use active comprehension strategies
- I **K.1.09.a** Derive meaning while reading
- I **K.1.09.b** Check reading understanding
- I **K.2.01.a** Brainstorm ideas with teacher/peers
- I **K.2.01.d** Use sources to gather information
- I **K.2.02.c** Write to inform
- I **K.2.08** Write across content areas
- I **K.2.09.b** Write/draw to express opinions
- I **K.2.11.a** Illustrate and/or write in journals
- I **K.3.03** Demonstrate spelling of English
- I **K.3.04.b** Logical words/appropriate word order

Lesson Planner CD-ROM
Develop and customize your own lesson plans with the Tennessee Lesson Planner CD-ROM

Blueprint for Learning Key:
A = Assessed, **I** = Introduced, **M** = Maintained or Mastered, **D** = Developing
SC = Science, **SS** = Social Studies

186510

Target Skills of the Week

Phonemic Awareness	Blending Phonemes; Segmenting Phonemes
Phonics	Initial Consonant: *Dd*; Words with Short *i* and Short *a*
Comprehension	Text Organization and Summarizing; Summarize
Vocabulary	High-Frequency Words; Using Opposites
Fluency	Phonics Library Decodable Text

DAY 3

Big Rig
by Amy Griffin
illustrated by Bob Kolar

K.1.04.a, K.1.04.g, K.1.07.d
Daily Routines, *T42-T43*
Calendar, Message, High-Frequency Words

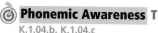 **Phonemic Awareness** T
K.1.04.b, K.1.04.c
Reading the Big Book, *T44-T49* K.1.06

Comprehension Strategy, *T45, T48*
Summarize K.1.09.b

Comprehension Skill, *T45, T46, T47*
Text Organization and Summarizing T K.1.08.b, K.1.09

Concepts of Print, *T46, T47* K.1.05.c, K.1.07
First/Last Letter in a Word; Matching Words T

Phonics, *T50* K.1.05.b, K.1.05.c
Review Consonant *d*;
Blending Short *i* Words T

Reading Decodable Text, *T51-T53*
"Big Rig" K.1.05.c

Vocabulary Reader K.1.07

Leveled Reader
K.1.04, K.1.05, K.1.09

Building Words, *T54* K.1.05.b, K.1.05.c, K.1.05.d
Words with Short *i*

Shared Writing, *T55* K.1.03.a, K.2.07, K.2.08.d
Writing About Signs

DAY 4

K.1.07
Daily Routines, *T56-T57*
Calendar, Message, High-Frequency Words

Phonemic Awareness T
K.1.04.b, K.1.04.c
Reading the Science Link, *T58-T59*
K.1.08.b, K.1.08.d, K.1.09
Comprehension Strategy, *T58* K.1.09.b
Summarize

Comprehension Skill, *T58* K.1.08.b, K.1.09
Text Organization and Summarizing T

Concepts of Print, *T59* K.1.05.c, K.1.07
First/Last Letter in a Word;
Matching Words T

Phonics, *T60-T61* K.1.05.b, K.1.05.c
Blending Short *i* Words T

Vocabulary Reader K.1.07

Leveled Reader
K.1.04, K.1.05, K.1.09

Building Words, *T62* K.1.05.b, K.1.05.c, K.1.05.d
Words with Short *i* or Short *a*

Interactive Writing, *T63* K.1.03.a, K.2.07, K.2.08.d
Writing About Signs

DAY 5

Wheels Around

The Wheels on the Bus

Look for Wheels

Big Rig
by Amy Griffin
illustrated by Bob Kolar

K.1.05.c, K.1.07.d
Daily Routines, *T64-T65*
Calendar, Message, High-Frequency Words

Phonemic Awareness T
K.1.04.b, K.1.04.c
Revisiting the Literature, *T66* K.1.09

Comprehension Skill, *T66* K.1.08.b, K.1.09
Text Organization and Summarizing T

Building Fluency, *T67* K.1.06

Phonics Review, *T68* K.1.05.b, K.1.05.c
Familiar Consonants; Short *i* Words T

High-Frequency Word Review, *T69* K.1.07.e, K.3.03
Words: *a, and, for, go, here, I, is, like, my, see, to* T

Vocabulary Reader K.1.07

Leveled Reader
K.1.04, K.1.05, K.1.09

Building Words, *T70* K.1.05.b, K.1.05.c, K.1.05.d
Words with Short *i* or Short *a*

Independent Writing, *T71* K.2.09.b, K.2.11.a
Journals: Favorite Type of Wheels

Concepts of Print lessons teach important foundational skills for Phonics.

Daily Lesson Plans

Managing Flexible Groups

Leveled Instruction and Leveled Practice

	DAY 1	DAY 2
WHOLE CLASS	• Daily Routines (TE pp. T24–T25) • Teacher Read Aloud: *Wheels Around* (TE pp. T26–T27) • Phonemic Awareness (TE pp. T28–T29)	• Daily Routines (TE pp. T32–T33) • Big Book: *The Wheels on the Bus* (TE pp. T34–T35) • Phonics Lesson (TE pp. T36–T37) • High-Frequency Word Lesson (TE pp. T38–T39)
SMALL GROUPS *Organize small groups according to children's needs.*	**TEACHER-LED GROUPS** • Begin Practice Book pp. 31, 32, 33, 34. (TE pp. T27, T29) • Introduce Phonics Center. (TE p. T29) • Leveled Reader	**TEACHER-LED GROUPS** • Begin Practice Book pp. 35, 36. (TE pp. T37, T39) • Write letters *D, d;* begin handwriting Blackline Master 160 or 186. (TE p. T37) • Introduce Phonics Center. (TE p. T37) • Leveled Reader • Vocabulary Reader
	INDEPENDENT GROUPS • Complete Practice Book pp. 31, 32, 33, 34. (TE pp. T27, T29) • Use Phonics Center. (TE p. T29)	**INDEPENDENT GROUPS** • Complete Practice Book pp. 35, 36. (TE pp. T37, T39) • Complete Blackline Master 160 or 186. • Use Phonics Center. (TE p. T37)

English Language Learners
Support is provided in the Reaching All Learners notes throughout the week.

Independent Activities

- Complete Practice Book pages 31–40.
- Reread familiar Phonics Library stories.
- Share trade books from Leveled Bibliography. (See pp. T4–T5)
- Use the Phonics Center and other Centers. (See pp. T22–T23)

DAY 3

- Daily Routines (TE pp. T42–T43)
- Big Book: *The Wheels on the Bus* (TE pp. T44–T49)
- Phonics Lesson (TE p. T50)

TEACHER-LED GROUPS

- Begin Practice Book pp. 37, 38. (TE pp. T49, T50)
- Write letters *I, i;* begin handwriting Blackline Master 165 or 191.
- Read Phonics Library: "Big Rig." (TE pp. T51–T53)
- Leveled Reader
- Vocabulary Reader

INDEPENDENT GROUPS

- Complete Practice Book pp. 37, 38. (TE pp. T49, T50)
- Complete Blackline Master 165 or 191.
- **Fluency Practice** Reread Phonics Library: "Big Rig." (TE pp. T51–T53)

DAY 4

- Daily Routines (TE pp. T56–T57)
- Science Link: *Look for Wheels* (TE pp. T58–T59)
- Phonics Lesson (TE pp. T60–T61)

TEACHER-LED GROUPS

- Begin Practice Book p. 39. (TE p. T61)
- Introduce the Phonics Center. (TE p. T61)
- Leveled Reader
- Vocabulary Reader

INDEPENDENT GROUPS

- Complete Practice Book p. 39. (TE p. T61)
- **Fluency Practice** Color and reread Phonics Library: "Big Rig." (TE pp. T51–T53)
- Use Phonics Center. (TE p. T61)

DAY 5

- Daily Routines (TE pp. T64–T65)
- Rereading (TE pp. T66–T67)
- Phonics and High-Frequency Word Review (TE pp. T68–T69)

TEACHER-LED GROUPS

- Begin Blackline Master 36. (TE p. T67)
- Begin Practice Book p. 40. (TE p. T69)
- **Fluency Practice** Reread the Take-Home version of "Big Rig."
- Leveled Reader
- Vocabulary Reader

INDEPENDENT GROUPS

- Complete Blackline Master 36. (TE p. T67)
- Complete Practice Book p. 40. (TE p. T69)
- **Fluency Practice** Reread a favorite Phonics Library or Leveled Reader story.

- Complete penmanship practice (Teacher's Resource Blackline Masters 160 or 186 and 165 or 191).
- Retell or reread Little Big Book.
- Listen to Big Book Audio CD's.

Turn the page for more independent activities.

Managing Flexible Groups   T21

Ready-Made for Tennessee

Independent Activities

Building Vocabulary

ELA.K.1.01.a, ELA.K.1.01.e,
ELA.K.1.01.f, ELA.K.1.01.g,
ELA.K.1.07.a, ELA.K.1.07.b

Center Activity 19

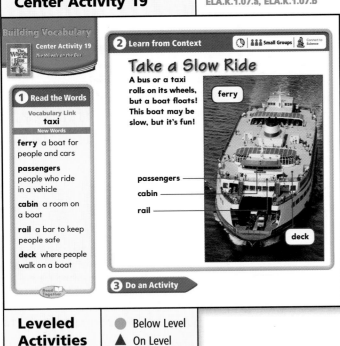

Building Vocabulary
Center Activity 19
The Wheels on the Bus

1 Read the Words

Vocabulary Link
taxi
New Words

ferry a boat for people and cars

passengers people who ride in a vehicle

cabin a room on a boat

rail a bar to keep people safe

deck where people walk on a boat

2 Learn from Context | Small Groups | Connect to Science

Take a Slow Ride

A bus or a taxi rolls on its wheels, but a boat floats! This boat may be slow, but it's fun!

ferry

passengers
cabin
rail
deck

3 Do an Activity

Leveled Activities on back of card
● Below Level
▲ On Level
■ Above Level

Reading in Social Studies

Independent Book
A Trip Across the Country
Students apply comprehension skills to nonfiction text.

A Trip Across the Country
by Ruth Adler
illustrated by Cindy Revell

SS.K.3.03.a, ELA.K.1.11.b

Center Activity 19

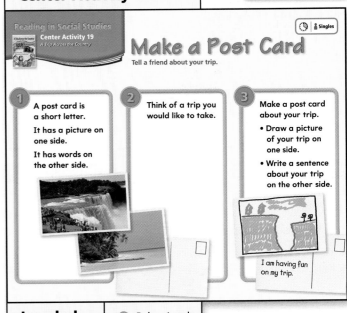

Reading in Social Studies
Center Activity 19
A Trip Across the Country

| Singles

Make a Post Card

Tell a friend about your trip.

1 A post card is a short letter.
It has a picture on one side.
It has words on the other side.

2 Think of a trip you would like to take.

3 Make a post card about your trip.
• Draw a picture of your trip on one side.
• Write a sentence about your trip on the other side.

I am having fun on my trip.

Leveled Activities on back of card
● Below Level
▲ On Level
■ Above Level

Hands-On Literacy Centers
The Wheels on the Bus

Challenge and Routine Cards

Read and Write Around the Room
① Walk and read.
② Write.
Share
Read to a friend.

1. A Bus Trip Book
Where would you like to take a bus?
TIP: Show the bus on the cover of your book.
Drawing Pictures of Places
• Make a list of places you would like to visit by bus.
• each place on your list.
Making Your Bus Trip Book
• Label each drawing.
• Make a cover with a title.
• Put the pages together into a book.
Sharing with Others
• Share your book with others.

Manipulatives

for

More Nonfiction Reading

30 topics aligned with Tennessee Science and Social Studies standards!

Setting Up Centers

Art Center

Materials
scissors, old magazines and catalogs, drawing paper, markers or crayons

Provide appealing materials in colorful, sturdy containers. Children will use them to create pairs of illustrations featuring red as *stop* and green as *go*. See page T41 for this week's Art Center activity.

Science Center

Materials
drawing paper, red and green crayons or markers

Children examine objects on display to look for wheels and figure out how the objects work. Then children cut out pictures of things with traditional wheels or round spinning parts and create a collage. See page T35 for this week's Science Center activity.

SS.K.1.02c

Writing Center

Materials
crayons, markers, lined and unlined writing paper

Children draw and label opposites pictures. Later they create and label drawings of everyday signs. See pages T31 and T63 for this week's Writing Center activities.

SS.K.1.02c

Day at a Glance
T24–T31

Learning to Read

Teacher Read Aloud, *T26*
Phonemic Awareness: */d/, T28*

Word Work

High-Frequency Word Practice, *T30*

Writing & Oral Language

Oral Language, *T31*

Daily Routines

Calendar

Reading the Calendar Tie the calendar routine into the theme. Use vehicle-shaped labels to mark special events. For example, a school bus could be used to mark the date of a class trip, or an airplane could mark a visit from someone's favorite aunt.

Daily Message

Modeled Writing Incorporate high-frequency words into the daily message. Call on children to spell these words for you as you write.

Bus 10 is here now. It got stuck today!

Word Wall

High-Frequency Words Have children clap to the spelling of each word on the Word Wall today: *t-o* spells *to*; *a-n-d* spells *and*; *h-e-r-e* spells *here*.

to	and	here

Word Cards for these words appear on pages R8–R10.

Daily Phonemic Awareness

Blending and Segmenting Phonemes

Read "To Market, To Market" on page 31 of *Higglety Pigglety.* Then play a blending game.

- I'll say some sounds. You put them together to make a word from the poem: /p/ . . . /ĭ/ . . . /g/ (pig).

- Now it's your turn to say each sound. Listen as I say the word slowly. Say *pig*, stretching out the sounds: *pĭĭĭg.* What is the first sound? (/p/) the middle sound? (/ĭ/) the end sound? (/g/)

- Continue, having children blend and then segment the sounds in *home* and *fat.*

- Now listen to this word: *bun.* Say the sounds softly to yourself and count them . . . How many sounds are in *bun?* What are they?

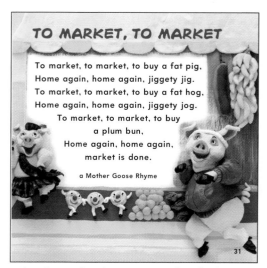

TO MARKET, TO MARKET

To market, to market, to buy a fat pig,
Home again, home again, jiggety jig.
To market, to market, to buy a fat hog,
Home again, home again, jiggety jog.
To market, to market, to buy
a plum bun,
Home again, home again,
market is done.

a Mother Goose Rhyme

31

Higglety Pigglety: A Book of Rhymes, page 31

Getting Ready to Learn

To help children plan their day, tell them that they will—

- listen to a story called *Wheels Around.*

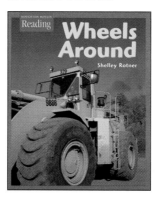

- meet a new Alphafriend.

- read, write, and learn about wheels in the Centers.

OBJECTIVES

- Develop oral language (listening, responding).
- Preview comprehension skill.

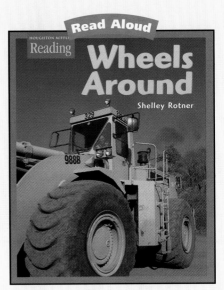

Wheels Around

Selection Summary This photo essay shows how useful wheels are and explains what different vehicles do.

Key Concept Kinds of wheels

Teacher Read Aloud

Building Background

Display *Wheels Around*. Read aloud the title and the author's and photographer's names.

- Ask children to name some objects at home or in the classroom that have wheels.
- Talk about wheels and some of the different ways wheels are used.

 COMPREHENSION STRATEGY
Summarize

Teacher Modeling Take a picture walk with children, and model the Summarize strategy.

Think Aloud The cover and title often tell what a book is mostly about. I think this book is about real things with wheels. As I read, I'll notice the important things about wheels. At the end, I'll tell those things in my own words.

 COMPREHENSION SKILL
Text Organization and Summarizing

Teacher Modeling Read aloud pages 2 and 3. Then model how to get the main idea from the text.

Think Aloud I was right. This book is about wheels. These pages tell me that wheels help us work and play. I'll remember: *wheels for work and for play.* Those words will help me remember the important things this book tells about wheels.

Listening to the Story

Point to the photographs as you read to help children connect the text with the photographs.

- As children may recognize many of the vehicles from their own experiences, allow time for them to enjoy the photographs.

- Pause occasionally to help children summarize what they've read about wheels for work or play. Encourage comments and questions.

You may wish to post an illustrated list of the vehicles from the story in the Writing Center to help children use the words in their writing and remind them of the ways wheels help us.

Responding

Oral Language: Summarizing the Story Help children summarize parts of the story.

- What are some of the ways wheels work for us? help us play?

- What kinds of wheels help us get around? Which help keep us safe?

- Which "wheels" were your favorite? Why?

Practice Book Children will complete **Practice Book** pages 31–32 during small group time.

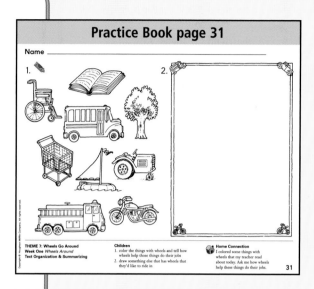

Practice Book page 31

Practice Book page 32

Book Center

• •

Make sure your Book Center is filled with books about many different kinds of wheels. Titles like *Curious George Rides a Bike* by H. A. Rey, *Sheep in a Jeep* by Nancy Shaw, *Wheels!* by Annie Cobb, *Window Music* by Anastasia Suen, and *Seymour Simon's Book of Trucks* are some good choices for the Center.

OBJECTIVES

- Identify pictures whose names begin with /d/.

Materials

- **Alphafriend Cards** *Dudley Duck, Fifi Fish, Keely Kangaroo*
- **Alphafriend CD** Theme 7
- **Alphafolder** *Dudley Duck*
- **Picture Cards** for *d, f,* and *k*
- **Phonics Center** Theme 7, Week 1, Day 1

Alphafolder *Dudley Duck*

Home Connection

Hand out the take-home version of Dudley Duck's Song. Ask children to share the song with their families. (See **Alphafriends Blackline Masters.**)

PHONEMIC AWARENESS
Beginning Sound

1 Teach

Introduce Alphafriend: Dudley Duck.
Use the Alphafriend routine to introduce Dudley Duck.

▶ **Alphafriend Riddle** Read these clues:

- This Alphafriend is an animal. His sound is /d/. Say it with me: /d/.
- This Alphafriend has feathers called down.
- He swims and dives for his dinner. He makes quacks!

When most hands are up, call on children until they say *duck.*

▶ **Pocket Chart** Display Dudley Duck in the pocket chart. Explain that Dudley's sound is /d/. Say his name, exaggerating the /d/ sound slightly. Have children echo you.

▶ **Alphafriend CD** Play Dudley Duck's song. Listen for /d/ words.

▶ **Alphafolder** Children name the /d/ pictures in the illustration.

▶ **Summarize**

- What is our Alphafriend's name? What is his sound?
- What words in our Alphafriend's song start with /d/?
- Each time you look at Dudley this week, remember the /d/ sound.

Dudley Duck's Song
(tune: My Bonnie Lies Over the Ocean)

Oh, look at the dandy duck, Dudley.

Dudley will dig all day long.

Dudley will dive in the water.

And Dudley will dance to this song.

❷ Guided Practice

Listen for /d/ and compare and review /f/ and /k/. Add Alphafriends *Fifi Fish* and *Keely Kangaroo* opposite *Dudley Duck*. Review each character's sound.

Hold up Picture Cards one at a time. Children signal "thumbs up" for words that start with Dudley Duck's sound, /d/, and a child puts the card below Dudley's picture. For "thumbs down" words, volunteers put cards below the correct Alphafriends.

Pictures: *dog, fan, kite, fork, desk, key, doll, king, fox*

Tell children that they will sort more pictures in the **Phonics Center** today.

❸ Apply

Have children complete **Practice Book** pages 33–34 at small group time.

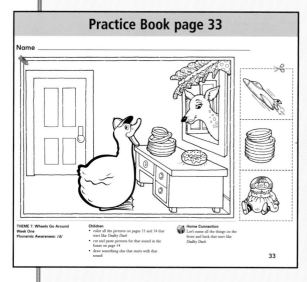

Practice Book page 33

Name _____

THEME 7: Wheels Go Around
Week One
Phonemic Awareness: /d/

Children
• color all the pictures on pages 33 and 34 that start like *Dudley Duck*
• cut and paste pictures for that sound in the boxes on page 34
• draw something else that starts with that sound

Home Connection
Let's name all the things on the front and back that start like *Dudley Duck.*

33

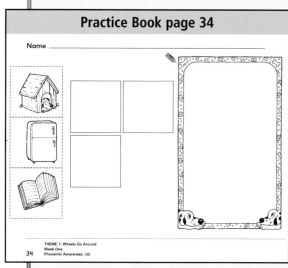

Practice Book page 34

Name _____

34 THEME 7: Wheels Go Around
Week One
Phonemic Awareness: /d/

ABC Phonics Center

Materials Phonics Center materials for Theme 7, Week 1, Day 1 ••••••••••••••••••••••

Display Day 1 Direction Chart. Children put *Dudley Duck, Fifi Fish* and *Keely Kangaroo* (without letters) in separate sections of Workmat 3. Then they sort remaining pictures by initial sound: /d/, /f/, and /k/.

PRACTICE

High-Frequency Words

Display Word Cards for the high-frequency words *I, see, and, go, to,* and *a* in a pocket chart.

- Call on children to identify each word and to match it on the Word Wall.

- Remind children that they will see these words often in books. I'll read a poem. You listen to hear if these words are in it.

- Read "Stop and Go" on page 30 of *Higglety Pigglety.* Did you hear some of these words in the poem? I did. Let's see which **Word Cards** you can match to the words in the poem. (*see, and, go*)

Higglety Pigglety: A Book of Rhymes, **page 30**

Have children write sentences.

- Display *I, to, go, a,* and add **Picture Cards** for *farm, zoo, goat, pig, lion,* and *seal.* Make a word card for *can* and help children read it.

- Ask individuals to use some of the cards to make sentences. Continue, adding the cards *see, and.* Children can then choose a sentence, write it, and add their own drawings.

ORAL LANGUAGE: VOCABULARY
Using Opposites

❶ Teach

Display page 6 of *Wheels Around*.

- Have children identify the old car and the new car on the page. Explain that words like *old* and *new* are called opposites. Write the words on chart paper.

- Continue the list by citing other story vehicles. Tow trucks pull cars. What is the opposite of *pull*? Cherry pickers lift things up. What is the opposite of *up*?

❷ Practice/Apply

Have children practice using opposites.

- Use a puppet to help children brainstorm opposites. Put the puppet *in* a box, then take it *out*. Put it *under* a table, then *on*.

- Read words on the chart and have children use them in oral sentences about objects in the classroom.

Writing Center

Put the chart in the Writing Center and ask children to draw their own opposites pictures. They can label their drawings, copying words from the chart or using temporary phonics spellings.

Day at a Glance
T32–T41

Learning to Read

Big Book, *T34*
Phonics: Initial Consonant *d, T36*
High Frequency Word: *for, T38*

Word Work

High-Frequency Word Practice, *T40*

Writing & Oral Language

Vocabulary Expansion, *T41*

Daily Routines

Calendar

Sunday	Monday	Tuesday	Wednesday	Thursday	Friday	Saturday
			1	2	3	4
5	6	7	8	9	10	11
12	13	14	15	16	17	18
19	20	21	22	23		
26	27	28	29	30		

Thursday will be Sunny

Reading the Calendar Share and discuss weather forecasts with children. Post what the weather is expected to be later in the week and have children check the weather when that day arrives.

Daily Message

Modeled Writing Write about something that happened yesterday. Compare yesterday and today on the calendar. Do this all week to help children with the concepts.

Yesterday we read about wheels. Today we will learn a song.

Word Wall

High-Frequency Words Today, children can take turns finding and naming Word Wall words as you spell them out.

to	and	go

Word Cards for these words appear on pages R8–R10.

🎯 Daily Phonemic Awareness

Blending and Segmenting Phonemes

Display **Picture Cards** *hen, pig, dog, cat,* and *goat.* Then play a blending game.

- I'll say some sounds. You put them together to name one of the animals. Listen: /h/ /ĕ/ /n/. (hen)

- Now it's your turn to say each sound. Say *hen* slowly, stretching out the sounds. What is the first sound in *hen*? (/h/) Listen again: *hen.* What is the middle sound? (/ĕ/) Listen again: *hen.* What is the last sound? (/n/)

- Continue, having children blend and then segment the other animal names.

- Finally, say *bug* and have children count and name the sounds in it.

Getting Ready to Learn

To help children plan their day, tell them that they will–

- listen to a **Big Book:** *The Wheels on the Bus.*

- learn the new letters *D* and *d* and their sound.

- discover ways to use wheels in the Science Center.

OBJECTIVES

- Introduce concepts of print.
- Develop story language.
- Reinforce comprehension strategy and comprehension skill.

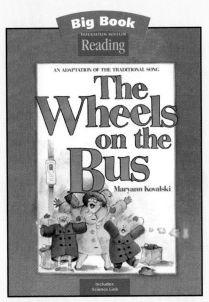

Big Book

HOUGHTON MIFFLIN
Reading

AN ADAPTATION OF THE TRADITIONAL SONG

The Wheels on the Bus

Maryann Kovalski

Includes:
Science Link

The Wheels on the Bus

Selection Summary A grandmother and her grandchildren sing a song about a bus as they wait at a bus stop.

Key Concepts

City buses, taxis

Waiting for a ride

English Language Learners

Teach children to sing "The Wheels on the Bus." Sing the first verse through once. Then sing it slowly, making sure children can hear the individual words. When children are ready, have them join in. Then ask children to listen for the words to the song as you read the story.

Reading the Big Book

Building Background

Read the **Big Book** title and the author/illustrator's name. Ask if children have ever sung "The Wheels on the Bus." Sing the first verse together or invite some children to sing for the class. See Theme Resources page R4 for music and lyrics.

Explain that this story includes the words of the song. Then have children tell what they know about buses.

Wheels Around was an information book about real wheels. But today's book tells a story about made-up characters. Identify Grandma, Jenny, and Joanna on the cover.

COMPREHENSION STRATEGY

Summarize

Teacher Modeling Model the Summarize strategy.

Think Aloud I know that when I read a story, I should pay attention to different things than when I read an information book like *Wheels Around*. With a story, I think about where the story takes place, who the characters are, and what happens to them. Let's do that with *The Wheels on the Bus.*

COMPREHENSION SKILL

Text Organization and Summarizing

Teacher Modeling Tell children that thinking about the topic and main idea can help them to remember new things.

Think Aloud Part of this story gives information about something in real life: a city bus. When I get to that part, I'll look for all the things that happen on a bus ride. Let's see what we can learn about real buses.

Big Book Read Aloud

Track the print as you read the selection aloud, emphasizing the rhythm and language pattern. On the pages from the song, pause to let children complete or supply phrases and ask what they have learned about a city bus.

Responding

Oral Language: Personal Response Encourage children to use the language of the story as they react to it.

- Were you surprised by the ending? Did you laugh? Do you think it was a good idea for Grandma, Joanna, and Jenny to take a taxi? Why?

- Do you think singing is a fun way to pass the time? What else could people do while waiting?

- What sounds do the wipers on the bus make? the horn? What was your favorite "bus" sound?

Science Center

Materials old magazines and catalogs
• drawing paper • crayons ....

Display items that have wheels or rotating parts. Include such things as an egg beater, wind-up toy, radio with knobs, and a game spinner as well as toy trucks and cars. Encourage children to examine the items and look for parts that turn. Then they can look for magazine pictures of things with wheels or rotating parts and cut them out for a collage.

Extra Support/ Intervention

Reinforce the concept of opposites by having children sing along and add motions as you reread the story. They can move *back* and *forth* for the wipers, hop *on* and *off* the bus, and go *up* and *down* as passengers.

PHONICS
Initial Consonant *d*

OBJECTIVES

- Identify words that begin with /d/.
- Identify pictures whose names begin with *d*.
- Form the letters *D*, *d*.

Materials

- **Alphafriend Card** *Dudley Duck*
- **Letter Cards** *d, p, r*
- **Picture Cards** for *d, p,* and *r*
- **Blackline Master** 160
- **Phonics Center** Theme 7, Week 1, Day 2

Dudley Duck's Song

(tune: My Bonnie Lies Over the Ocean)

Oh, look at the dandy duck, Dudley.

Dudley will dig all day long.

Dudley will dive in the water.

And Dudley will dance to this song.

❶ Phonemic Awareness Warm-Up

Beginning Sound Read or sing the lyrics to Dudley Duck's song and have children echo it line-for-line. Have them listen for the /d/ words and "duck" their heads for each one they hear. See Theme Resources page R2 for music and lyrics.

❷ Teach Phonics

Beginning Letter Display the *Dudley Duck* card, and have children name the letter. The letter *d* stands for the sound /d/, as in *duck*. When you see a *d*, remember Dudley Duck. That will help you remember the sound /d/.

Write *duck* on the board. Underline the *d*. This is the word *duck*. What is the first letter in the word? (d) *Duck* starts with /d/, so *d* is the first letter I write for *duck*.

❸ Guided Practice

Compare and Review: *p, r* In a pocket chart, display the **Letter Cards** as shown and the **Picture Cards** in random order. Review the sounds for *d, p,* and *r*. Have children take turns naming a picture, saying its beginning sound, and putting the card below the right letter. Tell children they will sort more pictures in the **Phonics Center** today.

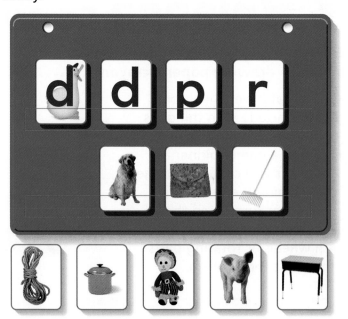

Penmanship Rhyme: D

Big *D* starts with a
long line down.
Go back to the top and
curve all the way around:
It's a *D*, a big *D*!

Penmanship Rhyme: d

Start in the middle.
Make a circle nice and round.
Go up to the top and
come straight down:
It's a *d*, a small *d*!

Penmanship: Writing *D, d* Tell children that now they'll learn to write the letters that stand for /d/: capital *D* and small *d*. Write each letter as you recite the penmanship rhyme. Children can chant each rhyme as they "write" the letter in the air.

❹ Apply

Have children complete **Practice Book** page 35 at small group time. For additional penmanship practice assign **Blackline Master** 160. Penmanship practice for the continuous stroke style is available on **Blackline Master** 186.

Practice Book page 35

ABC Phonics Center

Materials | Phonics Center materials for Theme 7, Week 1, Day 2 · · · · · · · · · · · · ·

Display Day 2 Direction Chart. Children put *Dudley Duck, Keely Kangaroo,* and *Fifi Fish* (with letters) in separate sections of Workmat 3. Then they sort remaining pictures by initial letter: *d, k,* and *f.*

OBJECTIVES

- Read and write the high-frequency word *for*.

Materials

- **Word Cards** *A, a, is, for*
- **Picture Cards** *bed, dog, leash, jam, jar, quilt*
- **Punctuation Card** period
- *Higglety Pigglety: A Book of Rhymes,* page 16

INSTRUCTION

HIGH-FREQUENCY WORD
New Word: *for*

❶ Teach

Introduce the word *for*. Tell children that today they will learn to read and write a word that they will often see in stories. Say *for* and use it in context.

This ball is *for* my dog.   I am late *for* dinner.   This letter is *for* you.

- Make sure children understand that the word *for* is different from the word and numeral *four*. Have them use *for* in oral sentences.

- Write *for* on the board, and have children spell it as you point to the letters. Say: Spell *for* with me, *f-o-r, for.*

- Lead children in a chant, clapping on each beat, to help them remember the spelling: *f-o-r, for! f-o-r, for!*

Word Wall Post *for* on the Word Wall, and remind children to look there when they need to remember how to write the word.

❷ Guided Practice

Build these sentences one at a time. Have children take turns reading each sentence.

Place the pocket chart in the Writing Center for children to build more sentences.

Display *Higglety Pigglety: A Book of Rhymes,* page 16.

- Share the rhyme "Baa, Baa, Black Sheep."

- Reread the last four lines of the poem, tracking the print and asking children to listen for the word *for.* Then ask children to point to *for* each time it appears.

Baa, Baa, Black Sheep

Baa, baa, black sheep,
Have you any wool?
Yes, sir, yes, sir,
Three bags full,
One for the master,
One for the dame,
One for the little boy
Who lives in the lane.

a Mother Goose Rhyme

16

Higglety Pigglety: A Book of Rhymes, **page 16**

❸ Apply

- Have children complete **Practice Book** page 36 at small group time.

- On Day 3 they will practice reading *for* in the **Phonics Library** story "Big Rig."

Practice Book page 36

Name _____

for

1.
I see a pan
a cat.

2.
I see a mat and a hat
a man.

3.
I see a van ____ Nan.

4.
I see a hat ____ Nan.

THEME 7: Wheels Go Around
Week One
High-Frequency Word *for*

36

Children
• for 1, 2, and 3, read the sentences and write the word *for* on the lines
• mark the smile (yes) or the frown (no) to show whether the picture goes with the sentence
• for 4, draw a hat for Nan and write the word *for*

Home Connection
I am learning to read the word *for.* Let me read these sentences to you. Then we could make up some more about Nan.

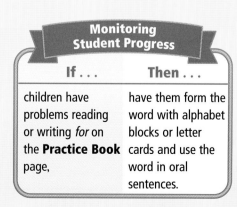

Monitoring Student Progress

If . . .	Then . . .
children have problems reading or writing *for* on the **Practice Book** page,	have them form the word with alphabet blocks or letter cards and use the word in oral sentences.

- Read high-frequency words.
- Create and write sentences with high-frequency words.

- **Word Cards** *A, a, and, for, go, is, to*
- **Picture Cards** *bike, boat, boy, girl, horse*
- **Punctuation Card** *period*

PRACTICE

High-Frequency Words

Tell children that you will build a sentence about things with wheels.

- Display the **Word Cards** and **Picture Cards** in random order. Then put the **Word Card** and **Picture Card** for *A* and *bike* in the pocket chart and read: *A bike.*

- I want the next word to be *is.* Who can find that word? Now who can read my sentence so far?

- Continue building the sentence: *A bike is for a girl.*

- Read the completed sentence together.

Have children write sentences.

- Children can write their own sentences based on one above. They might use their own names, substitute "wheels" of their own choosing, and add drawings.

- If children want to add new words, remind them to use what they know about letter sounds to spell the words (temporary phonics spellings).

VOCABULARY EXPANSION

Using Opposites

Listening/Speaking/Viewing

Review the opposites chart. Display the opposites chart children began yesterday and briefly review it.

- Ask if children can think of opposites from *The Wheels on the Bus* to add to the chart. Page through the book for ideas.
- Add children's suggestions to the chart. Whenever possible, have them dramatize the words.

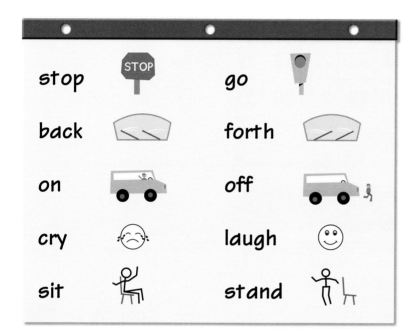

 **Center**

Materials drawing paper
red and green crayons or markers ....

Explain that red and green are not opposites, but that the colors *red* and *green* stand for the opposites *stop* and *go*. Write these words on separate sheets of red and green paper and place them in the Art Center. Children can create pairs of illustrations with a red label for *stop* (or *danger*) and a green one for *go*.

OBJECTIVES
- Use opposites.

Materials
- **Big Book** *The Wheels on the Bus*

DAY 2

VOCABULARY · WEEK 1

Vocabulary Support

The Vocabulary Reader can be used to develop and reinforce vocabulary related to the instruction for this week.

Vocabulary Reader

Trolley Ride
by Sarah Curran

 Challenge

Some children will think of other opposites to add to the chart. Challenge them to think of a single object that performs opposite actions. For example, wipers and swings go back and forth, seesaws and elevators go up and down, and lights go on and off. Children can draw and label pictures to show their ideas.

 English Language Learners

Although English language learners may not know both words in an opposite pair, they will know some words that have opposites. Encourage children to name words and have their English-speaking classmates provide the opposite.

Day at a Glance
T42–T55

Learning to Read

Big Book, *T44*

Phonics: Reviewing Consonant *d*; Blending Short *i* Words, *T50*

Word Work

Building Words, *T54*

Writing & Oral Language

Shared Writing, *T55*

Daily Routines

Calendar

Sunday	Monday	Tuesday	Wednesday	Thursday	Friday	Saturday
			1	2	3	4
5	6	7	8	9	10	11
12	13	14	15	16	17	18
19	20	21	22	23	24	25
26	27	28	29	30	31	

Reading the Calendar Recite the days of the week with children. Frame *Monday* and call on a volunteer to find the letter *d*. Say *Monday*, asking children to listen for /d/. Repeat for the other days of the week. Frame the word *day* in each day's name.

Daily Message

Modeled Writing
Try to use *d* words in the daily message. Call on children to point to and circle each *d*. Help children see that letters, like *d*, can appear in the beginning, the middle, or the end of a word, as in the sample shown.

Today we will design signs.

Word Wall

High-Frequency Words Choose a child to point to and read the new word that was added to the Word Wall this week. (*for*) Have children compare *for* to other words listed. For example: *for* has three letters like *see* and *and*; *for* has an *o* like *to* and *go*. Continue reading the remaining groups of words.

for	see
and	to	go

Word Cards for these words appear on pages R8–R10.

Daily Phonemic Awareness

Blending and Segmenting Phonemes

- Read "Hey, Diddle, Diddle" on page 32 of *Higglety Pigglety*. **Let's break apart some poem words. Listen: /h//ā/. Say those sounds with me. Now blend them: /h//ā/.** (hey)

- **Now I'll say another word from the poem. This time, you say it slowly to yourself and hold up a finger for each sound. Say** *see,* **stretching out the sounds.** Have children say and count the separate sounds. Continue, having children segment the sounds in *dish* and *moon*.

Hey, Diddle, Diddle

Hey, diddle, diddle!
The cat and the fiddle,
The cow jumped over the moon.
The little dog laughed
To see such sport,
And the dish ran away
With the spoon.

a Mother Goose Rhyme

32

Higglety Pigglety: A Book of Rhymes,
page 32

Getting Ready to Learn

To help children plan their day, tell them that they will–

- reread and talk about the **Big Book:** *The Wheels on the Bus.*

- read a story called "Big Rig."

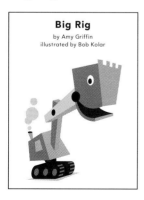

Big Rig
by Amy Griffin
illustrated by Bob Kolar

- take a bus ride in the Dramatic Play Center.

Reading the Big Book

OBJECTIVES

- Identify text organization and summarize text.
- Identify the first and last letters of a written word.

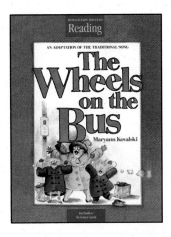

Reading for Understanding

Reread the story, emphasizing the rhythm. Pause for discussion points. Note that pages 8–9 show Piccadilly Circus in London, England. Point out the double-decker buses, which may be unfamiliar to children.

 Extra Support/Intervention

Help children see that this book is a story within a story. There is the story of Grandma, Jenny and Joanna shopping, waiting for the bus, singing, and missing the bus. The second story takes place on the bus, during the song. Page through the story to help children understand the sequence of events.

One day, Grandma took Jenny and Joanna shopping for new winter coats.

2

3

They tried on long coats and short coats, blue coats and red coats, plaid coats and even raincoats.

4

Joanna chose a coat with wooden barrel buttons. Jenny liked it too, because of the hood.

5

When it was time to go home, the bus didn't come for a long time and everyone grew tired. "I have an idea, sweeties," said Grandma. "Let's sing a song my Granny sang with me when I was a little girl." And so they began to sing. . . .

6

7

The wheels on the bus go
round and round
round and round
round and round

The wheels on the bus go
round and round
all around the town.

8   9

The wipers on the bus go
swish, swish, swish
swish, swish, swish
swish, swish, swish
The wipers on the bus go
swish, swish, swish
all around the town.

10   11

The people on the bus hop
on and off
on and off
on and off
The people on the bus hop
on and off
all around the town.

12   13

CRITICAL THINKING
Guiding Comprehension

pages 4–5

- **DRAWING CONCLUSIONS** Do the girls buy the first coats they try on? Why do you think that? (No. Coats are piled on the floor; the salesclerk looks tired.)

COMPREHENSION STRATEGY
Summarize

pages 6–7

Teacher-Student Modeling Review that to retell a story, readers think about the characters, where the story takes place, and what happens. Prompts:

- Who is the story about? Where are Grandma, Jenny, and Joanna when the story starts? (shopping) Where are they now? (at the bus stop) How do they pass the time? (They sing.)

COMPREHENSION SKILL
Text Organization and Summarizing

pages 8–9

Teacher-Student Modeling This is the part of the story that tells what happens on the bus ride. What can you learn about a bus from these pages?

CRITICAL THINKING
Guiding Comprehension

pages 10–11

- **CAUSE AND EFFECT** What part of the bus did we read about here? Why do the wipers swish?

Reading the Big Book   T45

CRITICAL THINKING
Guiding Comprehension

pages 14–15

- **DRAWING CONCLUSIONS** Are the people enjoying the ride? How do you know? (Yes. They are smiling.) Why might the driver toot his horn? (to warn people to get out of the way)

pages 18–19

- **CAUSE AND EFFECT** Why did the people go up and down? (Perhaps the bus hit a bump or the driver stopped suddenly.) Do you think the people should have been standing in the aisle? Why or why not?

 **COMPREHENSION SKILL**
Text Organization and Summarizing

pages 20–21

Student Modeling Ask what else children have learned about these old-fashioned buses. (Equipment: wheels, wipers, a horn) What job do buses do? (take people where they want to go)

REVISITING THE TEXT
Concepts of Print

pages 18–19

First/Last Letter in a Word
- Frame the word *and* and read it aloud. How many letters are in this word? (three) What is the first letter? the last? How do you know where the word ends? (There is a space after it.)
- Repeat with the words *bus* and *town*.

THEME 7: Wheels Go Around

The horn on the bus goes
  toot, toot, toot
  toot, toot, toot
  toot, toot, toot
The horn on the bus goes
  toot, toot, toot
  all around the town.

14   15

The money on the bus goes
  clink, clink, clink
  clink, clink, clink
  clink, clink, clink
The money on the bus goes
  clink, clink, clink
  all around the town.

16   17

The people on the bus go
  up and down
  up and down
  up and down
The people on the bus go
  up and down
  all around the town.

18   19

The babies on the bus go
waaa, waaa, waaa
waaa, waaa, waaa
waaa, waaa, waaa
The babies on the bus go
waaa, waaa, waaa
all around the town.

20

21

The parents on the bus go
ssh, ssh, ssh
ssh, ssh, ssh
ssh, ssh, ssh
The parents on the bus go
ssh, ssh, ssh
all around the town.

22

23

The wheels on the bus go
round and round
round and round
round and round
The wheels on the bus go
round and round
all around the town.

Grandma, Jenny, and
Joanna had so much fun . . .

24

25

CRITICAL THINKING
Guiding Comprehension

pages 20–21

- **MAKING JUDGMENTS** Are the people still enjoying their ride? Why not? (Babies are crying; people are frowning.) Would you like to be on the bus now?

pages 24–25

- **DRAWING CONCLUSIONS** What is happening now? (The story goes back to Grandma and the girls.)

REVISITING THE TEXT
Concepts of Print

pages 24–25

Matching Words

- Frame and read *bus*. Have children match *bus* elsewhere on the page. Matching words are spelled the same way. Frame and spell *bus* each time it appears. Repeat with *round*.

Challenge

Children who can easily match words in the text may be able to find and match phrases that repeat, such as "round and round." At small group time, have these children find matching phrases.

Reading the Big Book **T47**

CRITICAL THINKING

Guiding Comprehension

pages 26–27

- **CAUSE AND EFFECT** What happened because Grandma, Jenny, and Joanna were having so much fun singing? (They missed the bus.)

page 30

- **SEQUENCE OF EVENTS** What did Grandma, Jenny, and Joanna do next? (took a taxi)

COMPREHENSION STRATEGY

Summarize

page 30

Student Modeling Call on children to name the main characters. Ask: What important things did Grandma, Jenny, and Joanna do at the beginning of the story? (shopped, waited for a bus) in the middle of the story? (sang a song) at the end? (missed the bus, took a taxi)

Oral Language

taxi: A taxi is a car that gives you a ride somewhere. People pay the driver for taking them where they want to go. Explain how a taxi ride differs from a bus ride.

They missed the bus!

26

27

So . . .

28

29

They took a taxi.

30

Responding

Oral Language: Retelling

Use these prompts to help children retell the story:

- Why did Grandma take Jenny and Joanna shopping? Why did Grandma, Jenny, and Joanna begin singing?

- What things happened on the bus in the song?

- Why did Grandma, Jenny, and Joanna miss the bus? What happened at the end of the story?

- What does the story tell about a real, old-fashioned bus ride?

Oral Language: Literature Circle Have small groups discuss their favorite parts of the book. Would you have enjoyed riding on the old-fashioned bus in the song? Why?

Practice Book Children will complete **Practice Book** page 37 during small group time.

Practice Book page 37

Dramatic Play Center

Set up the Dramatic Play Center to resemble a bus. Children can line up chairs for passengers and have a special seat for the driver. They can create traffic signs and bus safety signs. Provide props for riders to use on the bus, such as dolls and packages. Have small groups of children visit the center to reenact the bus ride from the story or create their own bus-ride scenario.

Monitoring Student Progress

If . . .	Then . . .
children need more practice with topic and main idea,	help them review a nonfiction book's cover and title to see what the book is about.

OBJECTIVES

- Identify words with initial consonant *d*, /d/.
- Blend and read words with *a, b, d, f, g, h, i, m, n, p, r, s, t,* and short *i*.
- Learn academic language: *vowel* or *helper letter*.

Materials

- **Alphafriend Cards** *Dudley Duck, Iggy Iguana*
- **Letter Cards** *a, b, d, f, g, h, i, m, n, p, r, s, t*
- **Alphafriend CD** Theme 7
- **Blending Routines Card 1**

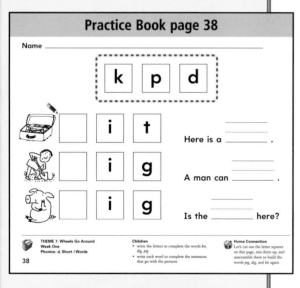

Practice Book page 38

Monitoring Student Progress

If . . .	Then . . .
children have trouble blending words such as *dig* or *pig*,	repeat this lesson using **Blending Routines Card 2,** *Sound-by Sound Blending.*

PHONICS
Blending Short *i* Words

❶ Teach: Connect Sounds to Letters

Review consonant *d*. Ask children what letter and sound they think of when they see Dudley Duck.

- Play Dudley Duck's song, and have children clap for each /d/ word.
- Write *D* and *d* on the board, and list words from the song.

Review short *i*. Tell children that they'll build a word with *d*, but first they'll need a vowel ("helper letter").

- Display Alphafriend Card *Iggy Iguana.* You remember Iggy. Iggy is an iguana. Say *Iggy Iguana* with me. Iggy's letter is the vowel *i*, and the sound *i* usually stands for is /ĭ/. Hold up the **Letter Card** *i*. Say /ĭ/. Listen for /ĭ/ in these words: /ĭ/ *if*, /ĭ/ *in*, /ĭ/ *itch*.

Model Blending Routine 1. Show the **Letter Card** *g* and review its sound. Tell children that they know all the letters to build the word *dig*.

- Show the **Letter Cards** *d, i,* and *g*. Have children identify each letter and the sound it stands for.
- Model blending the sounds as you point to each letter with a sweeping motion. I say the sounds in order: first /d/, then /i/, then /g/. I hold each sound until I say the next one, dĭĭĭg, *dig*. I've made the word *dig*.
- Repeat, having children blend and pronounce *dig* with you.
- Continue the process for the words *pig* and *big*.

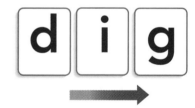

❷ Guided Practice

Check Understanding. Display the word *rig* and ask individuals to blend the word. For more practice, display *kit, fin,* and *ham*. Have children blend the words, modeling blending as needed. Continue as children blend *ran, tab,* and *man*. Have children read the sentence *I see a pig*, blending the sounds for *pig*. (Underlined words are from the Word Wall.)

❸ Apply

Children complete **Practice Book** page 38 at small group time.

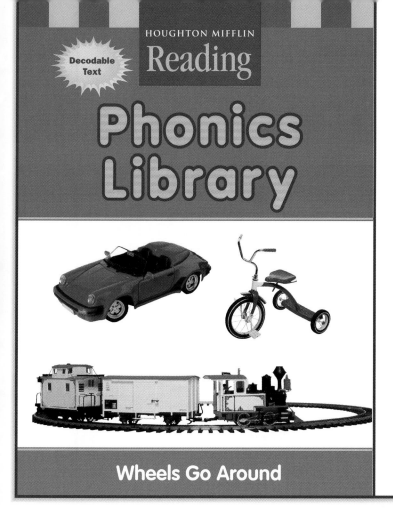

HOUGHTON MIFFLIN

Reading

Decodable Text

Phonics Library

Wheels Go Around

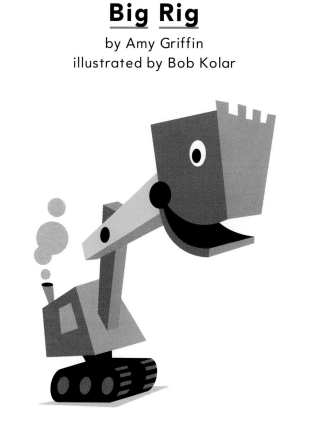

Big Rig

by Amy Griffin
illustrated by Bob Kolar

1

PHONICS LIBRARY
Reading Decodable Text

Phonics/Decoding Strategy

Teacher-Student Modeling Discuss using the
Phonics/Decoding strategy to read words in the story.

Think Aloud The first word in the title begins with capital *B*. The
sound for *B* is /b/. The next letters are *i* and *g*. I
blend the sounds to read this word, *Bĭĭg, Big.* The next word begins
with capital *R*. It also has an *i* and *g* in it. Let's blend the sounds to
read this word, *Rrrĭĭg, Rig.*

Preview the pictures on pages 1–2. Explain that a rig is a
type of machine. Ask children to predict what this rig will be
doing.

OBJECTIVES

- Apply the phonics skills to decode short *i* words.
- Apply high-frequency words.
- Reread for fluency practice.

Big Rig can dig.

2

Dig, dig, dig.

3

Prompts for Decoding

Have children read each page silently before reading aloud to you. Remind children to look at each letter as they sound out the word. Prompts:

page 2 What words rhyme with *big* on this page? What letters are the same in these words?

Oral Language

Discuss the story Remind children to speak in complete sentences.

- **What are Big Rig and Dan doing?** (building a house.)
- **How does Big Rig help Dan?** (Big Rig digs the pit so Dan can build the house.)

Identify short *i* words. Ask children to reread the story and identify short *i* words. Have them use these words to write sentences that tell about the story.

Build Fluency

Model fluent reading.

- Read aloud page 5. Then have children read the page aloud.
- Have children reread the same page several times until each child can read it aloud smoothly.

Word Key

Decodable words with short *i* ————

High-Frequency Words ————

Home Connection

Have children color the pictures in the take-home version of "Big Rig." After rereading on Day 4, they can read it to family members at home. (See **Phonics Library Blackline Masters.**)

T52   **THEME 7: Wheels Go Around**

Big Rig can dig a pit.

4

Big Rig can dig a pit for Dan.

5

Dan can .

6

Dan can .
Big Rig can dig.

7

OBJECTIVES

- Blend consonant sounds with short *i* to read words.

Materials

- **Letter Cards** *a, b, d, f, g, h, i, m, n, p, r, s, t, v*

PRACTICE

BUILDING WORDS
Words with Short *i*

Model building the word *dig*.

- Display **Letter Cards** *a, b, d, f, g, h, i, m, n, p, r, s, t,* and *v*.

- Using the **Letter Cards,** model how to build *dig*. First I'll stretch out the sounds: /d/ /ĭ/ /g/. How many sounds do you hear? The first sound is /d/. I'll up a *d* to spell that. The next sound is /ĭ/. What letter should I choose for that? The last sound is /g/. What letter should I choose for that? Blend /d/ /ĭ/ and /g/ to read *dĭ ĭ ĭg, dig*.

Model building words that rhyme with *dig*.

- Tell children you want to build a word that rhymes with *dig*.

- Replace *d* with *b* and say: Now what happens if I change /d/ to /b/?

- Continue making and blending short *i* words by substituting *f, r,* and *p*.

Word Wall Add *dig* to the Word Wall. Have one child point to the word *dig*. Remind children that they can use *dig* to help them read and write words that rhyme with *dig*.

Check Understanding Have children use letter stamps or other manipulatives in your collection to build short *i* words.

Extend Practice Ask children to build these words: *fit, ban, sit, fan, ham, vat, mad*. Display the sentence: *I like to dig*. Have children read it, blending the sounds for *dig*. Children should recognize the underlined words from the Word Wall.

English Language Learners

Listen for children's pronunciation of /ĭ/. Most languages have just one *i* sound. As a result, many English learners produce a lengthened vowel sound. Compensate by saying /ĭ/ somewhat faster and shorter than you ordinarily would.

SHARED WRITING
Writing About Signs

Observe signs. Take a brief walk around the school to observe signs. Upon returning to the classroom, help children record their observations.

● Organize these pairs of signs together on a chart, reviewing words that name opposites. Children might mention signs such as *in/out, push/pull, enter/exit,* and *boys/girls.*

● Help children brainstorm other signs they have seen. What signs might you see when you are crossing the street? in an elevator? in a school?

● Discuss the purposes of the signs, using prompts as needed. Where would you see this sign? Who would read it? How would it help them?

Use children's suggestions in a shared writing experience.

● Choose a scene to pantomime, such as driving a bus or crossing a street. Write about the event, having children suggest a sign they might see and what information it gives.

● Have children take turns writing about each scene and sign.

Signs

in	out
enter	exit
walk	don't walk
push	pull
boys	girls
stop	go

We are driving a bus.
We see a red sign.
It tells us to stop.

We are crossing the street.
We see a Walk sign.
It tells us we can cross safely.

English Language Learners

Make sure children know the meaning of signs around school and help them incorporate the words into their vocabulary. Take pictures of the signs to post in the classroom and use with children.

DAY 4
week 1

Day at a Glance
T56–T63

Learning to Read

Big Book, *T58*
Phonics: Reviewing Consonant *d*; Blending Short *i* Words, *T60*

Word Work

Building Words, *T62*

Writing & Oral Language

Interactive Writing, *T63*

Daily Routines

Sunday	Monday	Tuesday	Wednesday	Thursday	Friday	Saturday
			1	2	3	4
5	6	7	8	9	10	11
12	13	14	15	16	17	18
19	20	21	22	23	24	25
26	27	28	29	30	31	

Calendar

Reading the Calendar
Incorporate opposite words into your calendar routine. What day comes *before* Tuesday? What day comes *after* Thursday? The *first* day of the month was a _____. The *last* day of the month is a _____.

The first day of the month was a _____

The last day of the month is a _____.

Daily Message

Modeled Writing
Duplicate some of the words in the daily message. Call on individuals to find and underline words that are the same. See the sample shown.

Today we <u>will</u> look for <u>wheels</u>. Max <u>will</u> build something with <u>wheels</u>.

Word Wall

High-Frequency Words Distribute index cards for words on the Word Wall. Have children match their cards to the words on the Word Wall. After each match is made, have other children chant the spelling: *d-i-g* spells *dig.*

to	and	dig

Word Cards for these words appear on pages R8–R10.

Daily Phonemic Awareness

Blending and Segmenting Phonemes

Read "Stop and Go" on page 30 of *Higglety Pigglety*. Tell children you will break apart a word from the poem. Listen: /r/ /ĕ/ /d/. Now you say the sounds and then blend them to make a word. (red) Repeat with *and*.

- I'll say another word. This time you say it slowly and hold up a finger for each sound. Listen: *go.* How many sounds do you hear? What are they?

- Continue with *we, top,* and *stop.*

STOP and GO

The traffic lights we see ahead
Are sometimes green
and sometimes red.
Red on top, and green below;
The red means STOP,
the green means GO!

Green below — GO — GO — GO!
Red on top — STOP — STOP — STOP!

by Marie Louise Allen

Higglety Pigglety: A Book of Rhymes, page 30

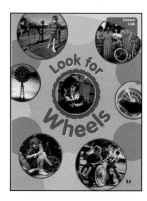 Getting Ready to Learn

To help children plan their day, tell them that they will—

- read the Science Link: *Look for Wheels.*

- learn to make and read new words.

- draw and write about signs in the Writing Center.

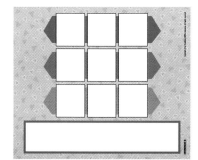

OBJECTIVES

- Identify text organization.
- Identify the first and last letter of a written word.

Oral Language

fair: Children may think of the word *fair* as meaning *just*. Explain that *fair* also names a place that has games and rides.

English Language Learners

Help children see that the commands *look for* and *find* have similar meanings. Use both in context to demonstrate meaning: *Look for two red crayons. Find the green book.*

INSTRUCTION

READING THE BIG BOOK
Science Link

Building Background

Did you see any wheels on the way to school today? Where? What did the wheels do? Display *Look for Wheels.* Read the title aloud, and discuss the pictures on the cover. Ask children what they think this selection will be about and why.

Reading for Understanding Pause for discussion as you share the selection.

COMPREHENSION STRATEGY
Summarize

page 34
Student Modeling Ask children what the selection has been about so far. *What have you learned about wheels?*

COMPREHENSION SKILL
Text Organization and Summarizing

Student Modeling *What does the first sentence on each page tell you to do?* (look for a wheel) *Wheel* is the topic. *What does each question ask?* (what the wheel does) What the wheel does is the important information.

Look for the wheel at the park.
What does it do?

Look for the wheel inside the car.
What does it do?

34

35

Look for the wheel in the cage.
What does it do?

Look for the wheel at the fair.
What does it do?

36

37

Look for wheels around you.
What do they do?

38

CRITICAL THINKING
Guiding Comprehension

page 34

- **MAKING JUDGMENTS** What makes this wheel turn? (the children pushing it) Which would you rather do, push the wheel or ride on it? Why?

page 36

- **CAUSE AND EFFECT** What makes the wheel on this page turn? (As the hamster runs, it turns the wheel.)

page 38

- **COMPARE AND CONTRAST** How are wheels being used differently in each picture?

TARGET SKILL
REVISITING THE TEXT
Concepts of Print

pages 34–35

First/Last Letter of a Word; Matching Words

- Frame the word *for* on page 34. How many letters are in this word? What is the first letter? The last letter?

- Direct attention to page 35. Who can match the same word on this page? Repeat with other pairs of words.

Responding

Oral Language: Summarizing Have children summarize the selection, using the pictures as prompts. What are some of the ways wheels can be used? How are all wheels alike? (They all turn around a center.)

REACHING ALL LEARNERS

Challenge

For children who are ready for a challenge, prepare cards for the words and end marks in one or two sentences from the selection. One child builds a sentence and then challenges a partner to read it, find it in the book, and add the correct punctuation card.

Reading the Big Book **T59**

OBJECTIVES

- Identify initial *d* for words that begin with /d/.
- Blend *d* and other initial consonants with short *i*.

Materials

- *From Apples to Zebras: A Book of ABC's,* page 5
- **Alphafriend Card** *Dudley Duck, Iggy Iguana*
- **Letter Cards** *a, b, c, d, f, g, h, i, k, n, p, r, t*
- **Picture Card** *dog*
- **Punctuation Card** *period*
- **Phonics Center** Theme 7, Week 1, Day 4
- **Blending Routines Card 1**
- **Teacher-made word cards** *can, pit*

Home Connection

Challenge children to look at home for items or for names that begin with the consonant *d.* Children can draw pictures to show what they have found.

PHONICS

Blending Short *i* Words

From Apples to Zebras: A Book of ABC's, page 5

Review consonant *d*. On page 5 of *From Apples to Zebras: A Book of ABC's,* cover the words with self-stick notes. Then display the page.

- Ask children to name each picture and tell what letter they expect to see first in each word and why.
- Uncover the words so that children can check their predictions.

Review short *i*. Remind children that to build words with *d*, they also need a vowel ("helper letter"), because every word has at least one of those.

- Ask which Alphafriend stands for the vowel sound /ĭ/. (Iggy Iguana)
- Display Iggy and have children think of other words that start with /ĭ/. (*if, igloo, in, itch*)

Review Blending Routine 1. Hold up **Letter Cards** *d, i,* and *g.* Watch and listen as I build a word from the Word Wall: /d/ /ĭ/ /g/, dĭĭg, dig.

Remove the *d* and put the **Letter Card** *b* in front of *ig.* Now let's blend this new word: /b/ /ĭ/ /g/, bĭĭg, big. Continue, having volunteers build and blend *fig* and *pig.*

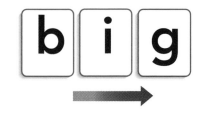

Check Understanding Display the word *rig* and ask individuals to blend the word.

For more practice, display *fit, can,* and *tin.* Have children blend the words, modeling blending as needed. Remind children to hold each sound until they say the next one, fĭĭt. Continue as children blend *had, fit, kit.* Display the sentence <u>My</u> pig <u>is</u> big. Have children read it, blending the sounds for *pig* and *big.* (Underlined words are from the Word Wall.)

Practice/Apply Use index cards to make word cards for *can* and *pit*. In a pocket chart, begin a sentence with the first two cards shown below. Say the words with children. For *dig,* ask what letter you need to spell each sound.

Repeat the activity with <**Picture Card:** *Dog*> *can dig a pit.* Tell children they will build more sentences in the **Phonics Center.**

- Have children complete **Practice Book** page 39 at small group time.
- In groups today, children will also read short *i* words as they reread the **Phonics Library** story "Big Rig." See suggestions, pages T51–T53.

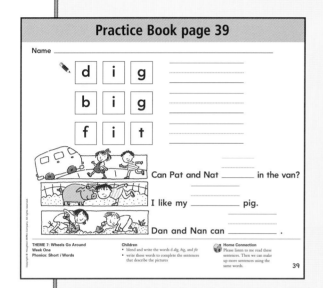

Practice Book page 39

Name _____

d	i	g	_____
b	i	g	_____
f	i	t	_____

Can Pat and Nat _____ in the van?

I like my _____ pig.

Dan and Nan can _____ .

THEME 7: Wheels Go Around
Week One
Phonics: Short *i* Words

Children
- blend and write the words *d*, *dig*, *big*, and *fit*
- write these words to complete the sentences that describe the pictures

Home Connection
Please listen to me read these sentences. Then we can make up more sentences using the same words.

39

Phonics Center

Materials Phonics Center materials for Theme 7, Week 1, Day 4 ....

Display Day 4 Direction Chart and Workmat 5. Children build short *i* words (*dig, pig, fig*) with **Letter Cards,** sound by sound. Then they use **Word** and **Picture Cards** to build the sentence *Dog can dig a pit.*

Challenge

Children who can easily build and blend short *i* words can write additional sentences for the words *big, dig, fig, pig,* and *rig.*

Monitoring Student Progress

If . . .	Then . . .
children have trouble building words,	have them work with you or a partner.

OBJECTIVES

- Blend consonant sounds with short *i* and short *a* to read words.

Materials

- **Letter Cards** *a, b, c, d, D, f, g, h, i, k, l, m, n, N, p, q, u, r, s, S, t, v*

BUILDING WORDS
Words with Short *i* or Short *a*

Model building the word *dig*.

- Display **Letter Cards** *a, b, c, D, d, f, g, h, i, k, l, m, N, n, p, q, u, r, S, s, t,* and *v.*

- Model how to build *dig* in a pocket chart. Have children listen to the word *dig.* Ask: How many sounds do you hear? The first sound is /d/. I'll put up a *d* to spell that. The next sound is /ĭ/. I'll put up an *i* to spell that. The last sound is /g/. What letter stands for that sound? Add the letter *g* to the chart.

Model building words that rhyme with dig.

- Replace the *d* with known consonants (*b, f, p, r*) to build other short *i* words. Have children blend each word. Keep a list of words you've built.

Model building the word *it*.

- Use **Letter Cards** to build *it.* Blend /ĭ/ and /t/ to read *it.* Ask which letter you should add to build *lit.*

- Model how to read *lit* by blending /l/ with /ĭ/ and /t/, *lĭĭĭt, lit.* Then replace *l* with *f* and say: Now what happens if I change /l/ to /f/?

- Continue making and blending short *i* words by substituting *b, h, k, p, qu, s.* Add the new words to your list.

Build words with short *a*.

- Blend /ă/ and /n/ to read *an.* Add initial consonants *c, D, f, m, N, p, r, t,* and *v* to build words.

Check Understanding Have children use magnetic letters or other manipulatives to build *dig* and *mat.* Model how to make needed corrections.

Extend Practice Have children build *Sam, fat, ham,* and *ran.* Exaggerate the final sound in each word to help children name the correct final consonant. Display the sentence <u>Here</u> <u>is</u> <u>a</u> fig. Have children read it, blending the sounds in the word *fig.* (Underlined words are from the Word Wall).

INTERACTIVE WRITING
Writing About Signs

Review signs and their uses.

- Remind children that signs have many uses. Elicit that many help us by telling us what to do.

- Show children pages 6–7 of *The Wheels on the Bus*. Ask: How do Grandma, Jenny, and Joanna know where to wait for the bus? (from the "bus stop" sign)

Write together to tell about signs.

- Display the chart from yesterday's Shared Writing. (See page T55.) Review the scenes and invite children to discuss what the signs tell.

- Continue adding sentences to the chart, for example: *We are waiting for a bus. We see a BUS STOP sign. It tells us where to stand.*

- If a suggested word begins or ends with a known consonant, have a child write the letter. Another child can write *for* or other high-frequency words. Choose someone to write the period at the end of each sentence.

Writing Center

Materials crayons • markers • lined and unlined writing paper • blank books

Put the chart paper from the previous activity in the Writing Center. Children "read" it on their own or with a partner. Each child can copy and illustrate his or her own sentence. Encourage children to show a sign in their drawings.

OBJECTIVES

- Use opposites in an oral context.
- Write letters or words for an interactive writing activity.

Materials

- **Big Book** *The Wheels on the Bus*, pages 6–7

DAY 4

WRITING

WEEK 1

REACHING ALL LEARNERS

English Language Learners

Take pictures of signs around town to add to school signs you photographed. (See the note on page T55.) Encourage children to make the environmental print part of their oral and written vocabulary.

Day at a Glance
T64–T71

Learning to Read

Revisiting the Literature, *T66*
Phonics: Review Consonants;
Short *a* or Short *i* Words, *T68*

Word Work

Building Words, *T70*

Writing & Oral Language

Independent Writing, *T71*

Daily Routines

Sunday	Monday	Tuesday	Wednesday	Thursday	Friday	Saturday
			1	2	3	4
5	6	7	8	9	10	11
12	13	14	15	16	17	18
19	20	21	22	23	24	25
26	27	28	29	30	31	

Calendar

Reading the Calendar Review any words you posted on the calendar this week. Have children suggest other events to note.

Daily Message

Interactive Writing
As you write the daily message and model how to write letters that stand for sounds, occasionally ask children to contribute words or letters they can read and write.

Brendon brought his favorite wheels to school today.

Word Wall

High-Frequency Words Read the Word Wall together. Then play a rhyming game: I'm going to find a word on the Word Wall that rhymes with *sit*. The word *it* rhymes with *sit*. Now raise your hand when you find a word that rhymes with *big*. (dig)

it	dig

Word Cards for these words appear on pages R8–R10.

Daily Phonemic Awareness

Blending and Segmenting Phonemes

Display the **Picture Cards** *bike, boat, jeep* and *jet*. Then play a blending game.

- I'll say some sounds. You put them together to name something for traveling: /b/ . . . /ō/ . . . /t/. (boat)

- Now it's your turn. Say *jet* slowly, stretching out the sounds. Have children count the sounds and identify the beginning, middle, and end sounds.

- Continue, having children blend and then segment *bike* and *jeep*.

Getting Ready to Learn

To help children plan their day, tell them that they will—

- reread and talk about all the books they've read this week.

- take home a story they can read.

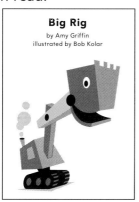

Big Rig
by Amy Griffin
illustrated by Bob Kolar

- write a story in their journals.

fig   pig
rig   big pig
dig

OBJECTIVES

• Review the week's selections.

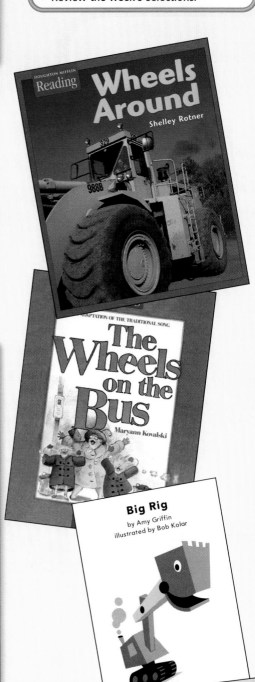

REVISITING THE LITERATURE
Literature Discussion

Review the week's selections, using these suggestions.

• Have volunteers display and tell about their favorite vehicle in *Wheels Around*.

• Sing the song from *The Wheels on the Bus*. Children can use the pictures from the book as prompts for the verses.

• Point to various photos from *Look for Wheels*. Select children to discuss what the pictured wheels do.

• Together, read "Big Rig." Ask individuals how they blended *dig*.

• Ask children to vote for their favorite book of the week. Then read aloud the winner

COMPREHENSION SKILL
Text Organization and Summarizing

Compare Books Remind children that the cover and title of an information book usually tell what the book is about. Explain that this is the topic of the book and that most of the sentences tell more about the topic. Browse through each selection with children, inviting comments about the topic and the main idea. Then help children develop a one- or two-sentence summary for each one, using the topic and main idea.

Rereading for Fluency

TARGET SKILL

Reread Familiar Texts Review **Phonics Library** books children have read so far. Remind them that they've learned the new word *for* this week, and that they've learned to read short *i* words. As they reread "Big Rig," have children look for words with short *i*.

- Feature several **Phonics Library** titles in the Book Corner, and have children demonstrate their growing skills by choosing one to reread aloud. Children can alternate pages with a partner.

Oral Reading Recognizing high-frequency words by sight helps children read more smoothly. Continue to provide daily practice with words on the Word Wall. You might want to send a word list home occasionally so that children can share their growing ability to recognize words.

Big Rig
by Amy Griffin
illustrated by Bob Kolar

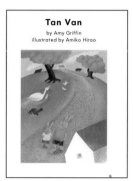

Tan Van
by Amy Griffin
illustrated by Amiko Hirao

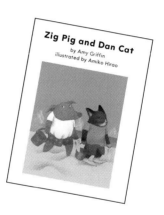

Zig Pig and Dan Cat
by Amy Griffin
illustrated by Amiko Hirao

Assign Blackline Master 36.
Children complete the page and take it home to share their reading progress. A copy appears on page R13.

My Reading Log

I can read

My new words

for   dig

Books for Small-Group Reading

The materials listed below provide reading practice for children at different levels.

Vocabulary Reader
Trolley Ride

Leveled Reader

The Parade

Little Big Book

Reading
The Wheels on the Bus

Little Readers for Guided Reading

Houghton Mifflin Classroom Bookshelf

Home Connection

Remind children to share the take-home version of "Big Rig" with their families.

<table>
<tr><td colspan="2">

OBJECTIVES

- Build and read words with initial consonants and short *i*.
- Make sentences with high-frequency words.

Materials

- **Word Cards** *a, and, for, go, here, I, is, like, my, see, to*
- **Picture Cards** *cat, dog, vet;* assorted others for sentence building
- **Punctuation Card** period

</td></tr>
</table>

TARGET SKILL

PHONICS
Consonants, Short *i* Words

❶ Review

Review building words with short *i* and short *a*. Tell children that they will take turns being Word Builders and Word Readers today. Have a group of Word Builders stand with you at the chalkboard.

- Let's build *dig*. First, count the sounds. . . . I know *d* stands for /d/. I also know that *i* stands for /ĭ/ and *g* stands for /g/. Write the letters.

- Children copy *dig* on the board and blend the sounds.

- At your direction, children erase the *d,* write *p* and ask the rest of the class (Word Readers) to say the new word.

- Continue until everyone builds a word by replacing one letter. Examples: *dig, pig, rig, fig, big; bit, sit, hit, kit, lit, pit, fit.* For a challenge, have the Word Builders change *fit* to *fan* and then *man, pan, ran, tan, van, can; cat, bat, fat, hat, mat, pat, rat, sat, vat.*

HIGH-FREQUENCY WORDS

a, and, for, go, here, I, is, like, my, see, to

❷ Review

Review the high-frequency words from the Word Wall.

- Give each small group the **Word Cards, Picture Cards,** and **Punctuation Card** needed to make a sentence. Remind children that the sentence begins with a capital.

- Children hold the cards and arrange themselves to make a sentence for others to read.

A		is	for	my		.

I	like	my			.

❸ Practice/Apply

- Children can complete **Practice Book** page 40 independently and read it to you during small group time.

- Have children take turns reading selections from the **Phonics Library** aloud to the class. Each child might read one page of "Big Rig," or a favorite **Phonics Library** selection from the previous theme. Remind readers to share the pictures.

- Use questions for discussion like the following:

- Do you hear any rhyming words? What letters are the same in those words?

- Find a word that starts with the same sound as Dudley Duck's name. What is the letter? What is the sound?

- This week we added the word *for* to the Word Wall. Find that word in "Big Rig."

Practice Book page 40

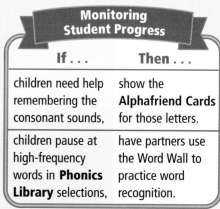

Monitoring Student Progress

If . . .	Then . . .
children need help remembering the consonant sounds,	show the **Alphafriend Cards** for those letters.
children pause at high-frequency words in **Phonics Library** selections,	have partners use the Word Wall to practice word recognition.

OBJECTIVES

- Blend consonants with short *i* and short *a* to read words.

Materials

- **Letter Cards** *a, b, c, d, f, g, h, i, k, l, m, n, P, p, r, s, t, v*

BUILDING WORDS
Words with Short *i* or Short *a*

Build words that rhyme with *dig*.

- Use **Letter Cards** to build *dig* in a pocket chart. Remind children to hold each sound as they say the next one, *dĭĭĭg*. Along the bottom of the pocket chart, line up the letters *f, p, r,* and *b*.

- Let's build a word that rhymes with *dig*. *Fig* rhymes with *dig*. Let's build *fig, fĭĭĭg*. Who can tell me which letter I should take from here to make *fig*?

- Take away the letter *d* and have a child replace it with the letter *f*.

- Continue building short *i* words, using initial consonants *p, r,* and *d*. On chart paper, keep a list of all the words you make. Reread the list together, blending the sounds.

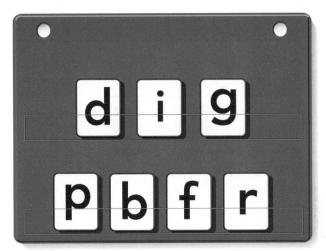

Build words with short *i* and short *a*.

- Continue building short *i* and short *a* words. Examples: *dig, pig, big, fig, rig; bit, fit, hit, kit, lit, pit, sit; can, fan, man, pan, ran, tan, van; bat, cat, fat, hat, mat, pat, rat, sat, vat.*

Check Understanding Have small groups work together to build short *i* and short *a* words with foam letters or other manipulatives. This time, they can add new words to the Word Bank section of their journals and add appropriate pictures.

Extend Practice Have children build words using *Pam, pin, cab,* and *lap*. Have children blend the words. Model blending as needed. Then ask children to read the sentence *I see a rig*. Remind them to blend the sounds for the last word. (Underlined words are from the Word Wall.)

INDEPENDENT WRITING
Journals

Preparing to Write

- Review what children learned about wheels so far. Point out the charts you made together, showing all the words for opposites that were used to tell about things wheels do and about signs that help people.

- Tell children that today they will write about their favorite type of wheels. Pass out the journals.

- What are some new words about wheels or vehicles you could put in your journals? What are some opposites you might use to tell about different signs and how they help drivers?

Writing Independently

- Remind children that they can use words from the Word Wall and this week's charts as they write. Children can also use temporary phonics spellings for words of their own choosing.

- If time permits, allow children to share what they've written with the class.

Portfolio Opportunity

Use self-stick notes to mark journal entries you would like to share with parents. Occasionally allow children to mark their best efforts or favorite works for sharing as well.

LEVELED READERS

WEEK 1

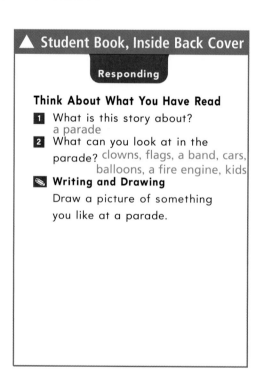

The Parade

Summary: *Everyone loves a parade! In this nonfiction book, readers are transported to a parade. They see clowns, flags, a band, cars, balloons, a fire engine, and children marching in the colorful parade.*

Story Words

Look *p. 2*

at *p. 2*

the *p. 2*

parade *p. 2*

are *p. 2*

High-Frequency Words

Review Words

Here *p. 2*

is *p. 4*

I *p. 8*

like *p. 8*

▲ ON LEVEL

Building Background and Vocabulary

Tell children that this story is about all the things that people enjoy seeing at a parade. Preview the photographs with children. Encourage children to share their own experiences watching parades and to talk about what they enjoy best about them.

Comprehension Skill: Text Organization and Summarizing

Read together the Strategy Focus on the book flap. Remind children to use the strategy and, as they read, to look for the important things about the parade.

Responding

Discussing the Book Have children talk about their personal responses to the book. Encourage them to talk about what they liked best about the book or what they found the most interesting. Have children point to sentences or photographs they enjoyed. Ask children to compare their ideas about things to see at a parade to the actual things shown in the photographs.

Responding Work with children to answer the questions on the inside back cover. Then help them complete the Writing and Drawing activity. Have children take turns sharing their drawings with classmates and explaining why they like that part of the parade best. Staple the pictures together to make a class book titled *We Like Parades*.

▲ Student Book, Inside Back Cover

Responding

Think About What You Have Read

1 What is this story about?
a parade

2 What can you look at in the parade? clowns, flags, a band, cars, balloons, a fire engine, kids

✎ **Writing and Drawing**
Draw a picture of something you like at a parade.

Building Fluency

Model Reread page 8 as children follow along in their books. Read the second sentence with strong feeling in your tone of voice. Write an exclamation point (!) on the chalkboard. Then have children find the exclamation point on page 8 and explain that this tells readers to use extra feeling when they read the sentence. Invite children to reread the page with you, imitating your tone of voice.

Practice Have children reread page 8 several times until each child can read it aloud smoothly and with strong feeling in the second sentence.

Oral Language Development

Parade Words Have children page through the story and pick out each word that names something they can see at a parade (*clowns, flags, band, cars, balloons, fire engine*). After they find each word on a page, have them point out that item in the photograph.

Practice Ask volunteers to pantomime each part of the parade as you reread the story aloud.

High-Frequency Words
Review Words: *Here, is, I, like*

Display the Word Cards for *Here* and *is*. Ask children to spell the words as you point to the letters in each word. Then have children turn to page 4 in the book. Ask them to listen for the words *Here* and *is* as you read the second sentence on the page. Ask children to take turns reading the sentence.

Next, display the Word Cards for *I* and *like*. Read the word s aloud. Ask children to listen for the words as you read the second sentence on page 8. Then have them turn to page 8 in the story. Point to the Word Cards and ask children to point to the words *I* and *like* in the text.

Here	is	I	like

Lesson Overview

Literature

HOUGHTON MIFFLIN
Reading

VROOM, CHUGGA, VROOM-VROOM

written by Anne Miranda
illustrated by David Murphy

Includes: Science Link

Selection Summary

Fast-paced, rhyming text describes the adventures of animal characters who compete in a great auto race.

1 Teacher Read Aloud
• *The Little Engine That Could*

2 Big Book
• *Vroom, Chugga, Vroom-Vroom*
Genre: Fantasy

3 Decodable Text
Phonics Library
• "Tan Van"

Tan Van
by Amy Griffin
illustrated by Amiko Hirao

4 Science Link

Cool Wheels!

This Link appears after the main Big Book selection.

Leveled Books

Vocabulary Reader

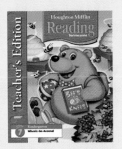

- Below Level, ELL
- Lesson

Leveled Reader

- On Level, Above Level
- Lesson
- Take-Home Version

Plus!
Online Leveled Books

Instructional Support

Planning and Practice

Tennessee Teacher's Edition

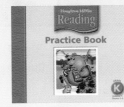

Teacher's Resources

Alphafriends

Practice book

Differentiated Instruction

Intervention/Extra Support

English Language Learners

Challenge

Ready-Made Centers

Phonics Center

Building Vocabulary

Reading in Science and Social Studies
- 30 books and activities
- support for Tennessee content standards

Hands-On Literacy Centers for Week 2
- activities
- manipulatives
- routines

Technology

Audio Selection
Vroom, Chugga, Vroom-Vroom

Curious George Learns Phonics

www.eduplace.com
- over 1,000 Online Leveled Books

Daily Lesson Plans

 Technology

Lesson Planner CD-ROM allows you to customize the chart below to develop your own lesson plans.

T Skill tested on Weekly or Theme Skills Test and/or Integrated Theme Test

Tennessee Curriculum Standards indicated in blue.

⏱ 60–90 minutes

Learning to Read

Phonemic Awareness

Phonics

High-Frequency Words

Comprehension

Concepts of Print

Vocabulary Reader
Let's Go!

Going for a Ride

Leveled Reader

⏱ 30–45 minutes

Word Work

High-Frequency Word Practice

Building Words

⏱ 30–45 minutes

Writing and Oral Language

Vocabulary

Writing

Listening/Speaking/ Viewing

DAY 1

K.1.03.a, K.1.07
Daily Routines, T80–T81
Calendar, Message, High-Frequency Words

⏲ **Phonemic Awareness** **T** K.1.04.b, K.1.04.c

Teacher Read Aloud, T82–T85 K.1.02

⏲ **Comprehension Strategy,** T82
Monitor/ Clarify K.1.08.b, K.1.09, K.1.11.b

⏲ **Comprehension Skill,** T82 K.1.09, K.1.13.i
Cause and Effect **T**

⏲ **Phonemic Awareness,** T86–T87 K.1.04.c, K.1.04.f
Beginning Sound /z/ **T**

Cross-Curricular Activity, T79 SS.K.1.02.c

Leveled Reader
K.1.04, K.1.05, K.1.09

High-Frequency Word Practice, T88
Words: *see, and, like, to, I, my* K.1.07.e, K.3.03

⏲ **Oral Language: Vocabulary,** T89
Using Position Words K.1.01.a, K.1.07, K.1.11.b

Vocabulary Reader K.1.07

DAY 2

K.1.03.a, K.1.07.d, K.1.07.e
Daily Routines, T90–T91
Calendar, Message, High-Frequency Words

⏲ **Phonemic Awareness** **T** K.1.04.c

Reading the Big Book, T92–T93 K.1.06

⏲ **Comprehension Strategy,** T92
Monitor/ Clarify K.1.08.b, K.1.09, K.1.11.b

⏲ **Comprehension Skill,** T92 K.1.09, K.1.13.i
Cause and Effect **T**

⏲ **Phonics,** T94–T95 K.1.05.b, K.1.05.c
Initial Consonant *z* **T**

⏲ **High-Frequency Word,** T96–T97
New Word: *have* **T** K.1.07.e, K.3.03

Leveled Reader
K.1.04, K.1.05, K.1.09

High-Frequency Word Practice, T98
Building Sentences K.1.07.e, K.3.03, K.3.04.b

Vocabulary Reader K.1.07

⏲ **Vocabulary Expansion,** T99 K.1.07, K.1.11
Using Position Words; Parts of a Car

Listening/Speaking/Viewing, T99
K.1.01.a, K.1.07, K.1.11.b

 Half-Day Kindergarten

Focus on lessons for tested skills marked with **T**. Then choose other activities as time allows.

Target Skills of the Week

Phonemic Awareness	Blending Phonemes; Segmenting Phonemes
Phonics	Initial Consonant: *Zz*; Words with Short *i* or Short *a*
Comprehension	Cause and Effect; Monitor/Clarify
Vocabulary	High-Frequency Words; Position Words; Parts of a Car
Fluency	Phonics Library Decodable Text

DAY 3

Tan Van
by Amy Griffin
illustrated by Amiko Hirao

K.1.01.i, K.1.04.b, K.1.04.f
Daily Routines, *T100–T101*
Calendar, Message, High-Frequency Words

Phonemic Awareness **T**
K.1.04.c

Reading the Big Book, *T102–T109* K.1.06

Comprehension Strategy, *T103, T104, T106* Monitor/ Clarify K.1.08.b, K.1.09, K.1.11.b

Comprehension Skill, *T103, T105, T107*
Cause and Effect **T** K.1.09, K.1.13.i

Concepts of Print, *T103* K.1.03.b, K.1.05.a, K.1.07
Matching Words; Using All Capital Letters **T**

Phonics, *T110* K.1.05.b, K.1.05.c
Review Consonant *z*;
Blending Short *i* Words **T**

Reading Decodable Text, *T111–T113*
"Tan Van" K.1.05.c

Vocabulary Reader K.1.07

Leveled Reader
K.1.04, K.1.05, K.1.09

Building Words, *T114* K.1.05.b, K.1.05.c, K.1.05.d
Words with Short *i*

Shared Writing, *T115* K.2.01.a, K.2.02.a, K.2.07
Writing a Class Story

DAY 4

Cool Wheels!

K.1.07.d, K.1.07.e
Daily Routines,
T116–T117
Calendar, Message,
High-Frequency Words

Phonemic Awareness **T** K.1.04.c

Reading the Science Link, *T118–T119*
K.1.08.b, K.1.08.d

Comprehension Strategy, *T118*
Monitor/ Clarify K.1.08.b, K.1.09, K.1.11.b

Comprehension Skill, *T118* K.1.09, K.1.13.i
Cause and Effect **T**

Concepts of Print, *T119* K.1.07
Match Words in Print **T**

Phonics, *T120–T121* K.1.05.b, K.1.05.c
Blending Short *i* Words **T**

Vocabulary Reader K.1.07

Leveled Reader
K.1.04, K.1.05, K.1.09

Building Words, *T122* K.1.05.b, K.1.05.c, K.1.05.d
Words with Short *i* or Short *a*

Interactive Writing, *T123* K.2.01.a, K.2.02.a, K.2.07
Writing a Class Story

DAY 5

K.1.04.e, K.1.07.e
Daily Routines,
T124–T125
Calendar, Message,
High-Frequency Words

Phonemic Awareness **T**
K.1.04.b, K.1.04.c

Revisiting the Literature, *T126* K.1.09

Comprehension Skill, *T126* K.1.09, K.1.13.i
Cause and Effect **T**

Building Fluency, *T127* K.1.06

Phonics Review, *T128* K.1.05.b, K.1.05.c
Familiar Consonants;
Words with Short *i* or Short *a* **T**

High-Frequency Word Review, *T129* K.1.07.e, K.3.03
Words: *I, see, my, like, a, to, and, go, for, have* **T**

Vocabulary Reader K.1.07

Leveled Reader
K.1.04, K.1.05, K.1.09

Building Words, *T130* K.1.05.b, K.1.05.c, K.1.05.d
Words with Short *i* or Short *a*

Independent Writing, *T131* K.2.09.b, K.2.11.a
Journals: Trains, Race Cars, and Other Vehicles

Concepts of Print lessons teach important foundational skills for Phonics.

Managing Flexible Groups

Leveled Instruction and Leveled Practice

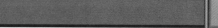

	DAY 1	**DAY 2**
WHOLE CLASS	• Daily Routines (TE pp. T80–T81) • Teacher Read Aloud: *The Little Engine That Could* (TE pp. T82–T85) • Phonemic Awareness (TE pp. T86–T87)	• Daily Routines (TE pp. T90–T91) • Big Book: *Vroom, Chugga, Vroom-Vroom* (TE pp. T92–T93) • Phonics Lesson (TE pp. T94–T95) • High-Frequency Word Lesson (TE pp. T96–T97)
SMALL GROUPS *Organize small groups according to children's needs.*	**TEACHER-LED GROUPS** • Begin Practice Book pp. 41, 42, 43, 44. (TE pp. T83, T87) • Introduce Phonics Center. (TE p. T87) • Leveled Reader	**TEACHER-LED GROUPS** • Begin Practice Book pp. 45, 46. (TE pp. T95, T97) • Write letters Z, z; begin handwriting Blackline Master 182 or 208. (TE p. T95) • Introduce Phonics Center. (TE p. T95) • Leveled Reader • Vocabulary Reader
	INDEPENDENT GROUPS • Complete Practice Book pp. 41, 42, 43, 44. (TE pp. T83, T87) • Use Phonics Center. (TE p. T87)	**INDEPENDENT GROUPS** • Complete Practice Book pp. 45, 46. (TE pp. T95, T97) • Complete Blackline Master 182 or 208. • Use Phonics Center. (TE p. T95)

English Language Learners Support is provided in the Reaching All Learners notes throughout the week.

Independent Activities

• Complete Practice Book pages 41–50.
• Reread familiar Phonics Library stories.
• Share trade books from Leveled Bibliography. (See pp. T4–T5)
• Use the Phonics Center and other Centers. (See pp. T78–T79)

DAY 3

- Daily Routines (TE pp. T100–T101)
- Big Book: *Vroom, Chugga, Vroom-Vroom* (TE pp. T102–T109)
- Phonics Lesson (TE p. T110)

TEACHER-LED GROUPS

- Begin Practice Book pp. 47, 48. (TE pp. T108, T110)
- Write letters *I*, *i*; begin handwriting Blackline Master 165 or 191.
- Read Phonics Library: "Tan Van." (TE pp. T111–T113)
- Leveled Reader
- Vocabulary Reader

INDEPENDENT GROUPS

- Complete Practice Book pp. 47, 48. (TE pp. T108, T110)
- Complete Blackline Master 165 or 191.
- **Fluency Practice** Reread Phonics Library: "Tan Van." (TE pp. T111–T113)

DAY 4

- Daily Routines (TE pp. T116–T117)
- Science Link: *Cool Wheels!* (TE pp. T118–T119)
- Phonics Lesson (TE pp. T120–T121)

TEACHER-LED GROUPS

- Begin Practice Book p. 49. (TE p. T121)
- Introduce the Phonics Center. (TE p. T121)
- Leveled Reader
- Vocabulary Reader

INDEPENDENT GROUPS

- Complete Practice Book p. 49. (TE p. T121)
- **Fluency Practice** Color and reread Phonics Library: "Tan Van." (TE pp. T111–T113)
- Use Phonics Center. (TE p. T121)

DAY 5

- Daily Routines (TE pp. T124–T125)
- Rereading (TE pp. T126–T127)
- Phonics and High-Frequency Word Review (TE pp. T128–T129)

TEACHER-LED GROUPS

- Begin Blackline Master 36. (TE p. T127)
- Begin Practice Book p. 50. (TE p. T129)
- **Fluency Practice** Reread the Take-Home version of "Tan Van."
- Leveled Reader
- Vocabulary Reader

INDEPENDENT GROUPS

- Complete Blackline Master 36. (TE p. T127)
- Complete Practice Book p. 50. (TE p. T129)
- **Fluency Practice** Reread a favorite Phonics Library or Leveled Reader story.

- Complete penmanship practice (Teacher's Resource Blackline Masters 182 or 208 and 165 or 191).
- Retell or reread Little Big Books.
- Listen to Big Book Audio CD's.

Turn the page for more independent activities.

Managing Flexible Groups   T77

Ready-Made for Tennessee

Building Vocabulary

Center Activity 20

ELA.K.1.01.a, ELA.K.1.01.e,
ELA.K.1.01.f, ELA.K.1.01.g,
ELA.K.1.07.a, ELA.K.1.07.b

Building Vocabulary
Center Activity 20
Vroom, Chugga,
Vroom-Vroom

2 Learn from Context ⏱ 👥 Small Groups | Connect to Science

3, 2, 1... Blast Off!
Race cars go fast, but the space shuttle goes faster. Zoom!

rocket
shuttle
tower
launch
pad

1 Read the Words

Vocabulary Link
zoom
New Words

tower a tall building

rocket something that goes very fast

shuttle a ship that rides on something else before flying into space

launch lift off the ground to fly

pad a flat base that things sit on

3 Do an Activity

Leveled Activities
on back of card
- ● Below Level
- ▲ On Level
- ■ Above Level

Hands-On Literacy Centers
Vroom, Chugga, Vroom-Vroom

Challenge and Routine Cards

Independent Reading
① Read a book.
② Draw and write.

Share
Show a friend.

1. Start Your Engine!
Write your own version of a car race.

Planning Your Story
• ___ pictures to show your ideas.
• What will happen to each car in your story? Why?

Telling Your Story
• ___ the beginning, middle, and end of your story.
• ___ sentences about your pictures.

TIP
• Include details in your pictures.

Completing and Sharing Your Story
• Create a cover and a title for your story.
• Staple the pages together.
• Share your story with classmates.

Manipulatives

have

Reading in Social Studies

Independent Book
Flags Everywhere!
Students apply comprehension skills to nonfiction text.

Flags Everywhere!
by Kathleen Gilson

SS.K.4.04.a, ELA.K.1.09.b.4

Center Activity 20

Reading in Social Studies
Center Activity 20
Flags Everywhere!

⏱ 👥 Small Groups

Flag Painting
We can make a flag.

1. See this flag. What does it look like?

2. Paint a big American flag.

3. Look at your flag. What do you think of? Talk with your friends about it.

Leveled Activities
on back of card
- ● Below Level
- ▲ On Level
- ■ Above Level

More Nonfiction Reading

School Days Long Ago and Today

Fun and Games

Save Our Tree
by Leslie Sullivan

Am Water
by K. G. Amonde

30 topics aligned with Tennessee Science and Social Studies standards!

Setting Up Centers

Science
Center

Materials
sheet of cardboard, toy cars, blocks, yardstick

Children experiment with releasing a toy car down a cardboard ramp. They change the slope and see how far the car travels each time. For a challenge, have children record the information and report to the class. See page T93 for this week's Science Center activity.

SS.K.1.02c

Math
Center

Materials
Wheels Around, counters, self-stick notes

Children look at the pictures of vehicles in the book and use counters to figure out the number of wheels shown in each picture. See page T109 for this week's Math Center activity.

SS.K.1.02c

Writing
Center

Materials
crayons, markers, lined and unlined writing paper

Children write or dictate a position word as a label for an illustration. Then they illustrate a group-written story, and their drawings are bound together in a book. See pages T89 and T123 for this week's Writing Center activities.

Day at a Glance
T80–T89

Learning to Read

Teacher Read Aloud, *T82*
Phonemic Awareness: /z/, *T86*

Word Work

High-Frequency Word Practice, *T88*

Writing & Oral Language

Oral Language, *T89*

Daily Routines

Sunday	Monday	Tuesday	Wednesday	Thursday	Friday	Saturday
			1	2	3	4
5	6	7	8	9		11
12	13	14	15	16	17	18
19	20		22	23	24	25
26	27	28	29	30	31	

Calendar

Reading the Calendar To tie the calendar routine into the theme, have children suggest vehicle-shaped labels to mark the weather. For example, use a snowplow outline for a snowy day or a windshield with wipers for rainy weather.

Daily Message

Modeled Writing
Incorporate high-frequency words into the daily message. Call on children to spell these words for you as you write.

Miss Rossi is here for music class. We want to sing "The Wheels on the Bus."

Word Wall

High-Frequency Words Have children chant the spelling of each word on the Word Wall today: *f-o-r* spells *for; s-e-e* spells *see; m-y* spells *my*.

for	see	my

Word Cards for these words appear on pages R8–R10.

Daily Phonemic Awareness

Blending and Segmenting Phonemes

- Say: I'm thinking of a word. I'll say some sounds, and you put them together to guess my word: /u/. . . /p/. (up). Continue, helping children blend sounds for *stop, go, van,* and *bus.*

- Now I'll say a whole word. This time, you say each sound to your partner. Say *bike,* stretching out the sounds. After partners confer, call on them to say and count the separate sounds. (/b/ /ī/ /k/) Continue with *boat, jet* and *plane.*

To help children plan their day, tell them that they will—

- listen to a story called *The Little Engine That Could.*

- meet a new Alphafriend.

- act out a story in the Dramatic Play Center.

OBJECTIVES

- Develop oral language (listening, responding).
- Preview comprehension skill.

Read Aloud

The Little Engine That Could

Selection Summary This classic tale tells of a little engine who believed in herself and succeeded in doing a big job.

Key Concepts

Trains, types of engines

Trying hard

Teacher Read Aloud

Building Background

Display Teacher's Edition page T84. Read aloud the title and the author's name and the illustrators' names.

- Ask children who have seen or ridden on a train to tell about it. Where on a train can you find the engine? What is the engine's job? (to pull the train)

- Have children tell how trains are similar to and different from some of the vehicles in *Wheels Around*.

 COMPREHENSION STRATEGY

Monitor/Clarify

Teacher Modeling Explain that sometimes readers or listeners come to something they don't understand in a story. Model the Monitor/Clarify strategy.

> **Think Aloud**

- So far I've read the title, *The Little Engine That Could*. I'm a little confused: What is it that the Little Engine could do?

- What I should do is read on and look at the picture to see if my question is answered. As I read, listen and see if you can find out what the engine could do.

 COMPREHENSION SKILL

Cause and Effect

Teacher Modeling Model how to identify cause-effect relationships.

> **Think Aloud** Sometimes in a story, one thing happens and causes something else to happen. As I read, I'll think about what happens and what causes it. You think about why things happen, too.

Listening to the Story

Fold your Teacher's Edition so that children can see page T85 as you read. Note that the art is also available on the back of the Theme Poster.

Read the story dramatically to help give life to all the characters. Use a rhythmic cadence to read the "I can not," "I think I can," and "I thought I could," refrains to emulate the sound of a train's engine. You might have children chant with you.

Responding

Oral Language: Summarizing the Story Duplicate and cut out the pictures on **Blackline Masters 104–105** and attach felt to the back of each one. With yarn, outline a "mountain" on a flannelboard. As children summarize the story, add the pictures to the scene.

- Who was on the little train? Where were they going?
- What kind of help did the little train need? Who did the dolls and toys on the train ask for help?
- Which engine was your favorite? Why?

Children may enjoy other stories in which hard work and determination pay off. Share other titles with children such as *Mike Mulligan and His Steam Shovel* by Virginia Lee Burton, *Little Toot* by Hardie Gramatsky, or a version of *The Little Red Hen*.

Practice Book Children will complete **Practice Book** pages 41–42 during small group time.

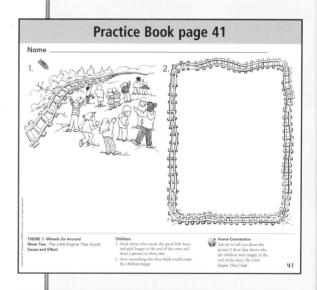

Practice Book page 41

Dramatic Play Center

Place a wagon loaded with toys in the Center. Children can then re-enact the story, making up conversations between the little train with the "load of toys" and the other engines.

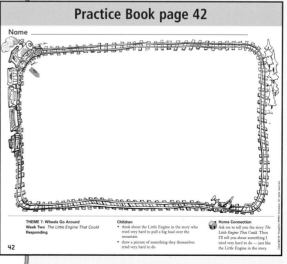

Practice Book page 42

The Little Engine That Could

Retold by Watty Piper

Illustration by George and Doris Hauman

Chug, chug, chug. Puff, puff, puff. Ding-dong, ding-dong. The little train rumbled over tracks.

She was a happy little train for she had such a jolly load to carry. Her cars were filled full of good things for boys and girls.

There were toy animals—giraffes with long necks, Teddy bears with almost no necks at all, and even a baby elephant. Then there were dolls—dolls with blue eyes and yellow curls, dolls with brown eyes and brown bobbed heads, and the funniest little toy clown you ever saw.

And there were cars full of toy engines, airplanes, tops, jack-knives, picture puzzles, books, and every kind of thing boys or girls could want.

But that was not all. Some of the cars were filled with all sorts of good things for boys and girls to eat—big golden oranges, red-cheeked apples, bottles of creamy milk for their breakfasts, fresh spinach for their dinners, peppermint drops, and lollipops for after-meal treats. The little train was carrying all these wonderful things to the good little boys and girls on the other side of the mountain.

She puffed along merrily. Then all of a sudden she stopped with a jerk. She simply could not go another inch. She tried and she tried, but her wheels would not turn. **(Ask: Why do you think the little train couldn't go another inch?)**

What were all those good little boys and girls on the other side of the mountain going to do without the wonderful toys to play with and the good food to eat?

"Here comes a shiny new engine," said the funny little clown who jumped out of the train.

"Let us ask him to help us."

So all the dolls and toys cried out together, "Please, Shiny New Engine, won't you please pull our train over the mountain? Our engine has broken down, and the boys and girls on the other side won't have any toys to play with or good food to eat unless you help us." **(Say: The dolls have flagged down another train. What happened in this story that made them do that? Do you think the Shiny New Engine will help?)**

But the Shiny New Engine snorted: "I pull you? I am a Passenger Engine. I have just carried a fine big train over the mountain, with more cars than you ever dreamed of. My train had sleeping cars, with comfortable berths; a dining car where waiters bring whatever hungry people want to eat; and parlor cars in which people sit in soft armchairs and look out of big plate-glass windows. I pull the likes of you? Indeed not!"

And off he steamed to the roundhouse, where engines live when they are not busy. How sad the little train and all the dolls and toys felt!

Then the little clown called out, "The Passenger Engine is not the only one in the world. Here is another engine coming, a great big strong one. Let us ask him to help us."

The little toy clown waved his flag and the big strong engine came to a stop.

"Please, oh, please, Big Engine," cried all the dolls and toys together. "Won't you please pull our train over the mountain? Our engine has broken down, and the good little boys and girls on the other side won't have any toys to play with or good food to eat unless you help us."

But the Big Strong Engine bellowed: "I am a Freight Engine. I have just pulled a big train loaded with big machines over the mountain. These machines print books and newspapers for grown-ups to read. I am a very important engine indeed. I won't pull the likes of you!" And the Freight Engine puffed off indignantly to the roundhouse. **(Say: Let's name the engines that would not help so far: The Shiny New Passenger Engine and the Big Strong Freight Engine. Why do you think they wouldn't help?)**

The little train and all the dolls and toys were very sad.

"Cheer up," cried the little toy clown. "The Freight Engine is not the only one in the world. Here comes another. He looks very old and tired, but our train is so little, perhaps he can help us."

So the little toy clown waved his flag and the dingy, rusty old engine stopped.

"Please, Kind Engine," cried all the dolls and toys together. "Won't you please pull our train over the mountain? Our engine has broken down, and the boys and girls on the other side won't have any toys to play with or good food to eat unless you help us."

But the Rusty Old Engine sighed, "I am so tired. I must rest my weary wheels. I cannot pull even so little a train as yours over the mountain. I can not. I can not. I can not."

And off he rumbled to the roundhouse chugging, "I can not. I can not. I can not."

(Ask: Who remembers the story title? Have we met the little engine in the title yet? Let's read on to find out what kind of engine it is.)

Then indeed the little train was very, very sad, and the dolls and toys were ready to cry. But the little clown called out, "Here is another engine coming, a little blue engine, a very little one, maybe she will help us."

The very little engine came chug, chugging merrily along. When she saw the toy clown's flag, she stopped quickly.

"What's the matter, my friends?" she asked kindly.

"Oh, Little Blue Engine," cried the dolls and toys. "Will you pull us over the mountain? Our engine has broken down, and the good boys and girls on the other side won't have any toys to play with or good food to eat, unless you help us. Please, please help us, Little Blue Engine."

"I'm not very big," said the Little Blue Engine. "They use me only for switching trains in the yard. I have never been over the mountain."

"But we must get over the mountain before the children awake," said all the dolls and the toys.

The very little engine looked up and saw the tears in the dolls' eyes. And she thought of the good little boys and girls on the other side of the mountain who would not have any toys or good food unless she helped.

Then she said, "I think I can. I think I can. I think I can." And she hitched herself to the little train. **(Ask:** How is what the Little Blue Engine said different from what the Rusty Old Engine said? Do you think she can? Let's listen and find out.)

She tugged and pulled and pulled and tugged and slowly, slowly, slowly they started off. The toy clown jumped aboard and all the dolls and the animals began to smile and cheer.

Puff, puff, chug, chug, went the Little Blue Engine. "I think I can—I think I can—I think I can—I think I can—I think I can—I think I can—I think I can—I think I can—I think I can."

Up, up, up. Faster and faster and faster the little engine climbed, until at last they reached the top of the mountain.

Down in the valley lay the city.

"Hurray, hurray," cried the funny little clown and all the dolls and toys. "The good little boys and girls in the city will be happy because you helped us, Kind Little Blue Engine."

And the Little Blue Engine smiled and seemed to say as she puffed steadily down the mountain . . .

"I thought I could. I thought I could. I thought I could. I thought I could. I thought I could. I thought I could. **(Ask:** Why do you think the Little Blue Engine was able to do such a hard job?)

Teacher Read Aloud

PHONEMIC AWARENESS

WEEK 2

OBJECTIVES

- Identify pictures whose names begin with /z/.

Materials

- **Alphafriend Cards** *Larry Lion, Pippa Pig, Zelda Zebra*
- **Alphafriend CD** Theme 7
- **Alphafolder** *Zelda Zebra*
- **Picture Cards** for *z, p,* and *l*
- **Phonics Center** Theme 7, Week 2, Day 1

Alphafolder *Zelda Zebra*

Home Connection

Hand out the take-home version of Zelda Zebra's Song. Ask children to share the song with their families. (See **Alphafriends Blackline Masters**.)

English Language Learners

Check to make sure children are voicing /z/. As needed, have them place their fingers against their throats to feel the vibration. Ask children to exaggerate the buzzing sound of /z/ to ensure contrast with /s/.

PHONEMIC AWARENESS
Beginning Sound

❶ Teach

Introduce Alphafriend: Zelda Zebra.
Use the Alphafriend routine to introduce Zelda Zebra.

▶ **Alphafriend Riddle** Read these clues:

- This Alphafriend is an animal. Her sound is /z/. Say it with me: /z/.
- You might see this Alphafriend in a *zzzoo.*
- She looks like a horse with black and white stripes.

When most hands are up, call on children until they say *zebra.*

▶ **Pocket Chart** Display Zelda Zebra in the pocket chart. Explain that Zelda's sound is /z/. Say her name, exaggerating the /z/ sound slightly. Have children echo you.

▶ **Alphafriend CD** Play Zelda Zebra's song. Listen for /z/ words.

▶ **Alphafolder** Children name the /z/ pictures in the illustration.

▶ **Summarize**

- What is our Alphafriend's name? What is her sound?
- What words in our Alphafriend's song start with /z/?
- Each time you look at Zelda this week, remember the /z/ sound.

Zelda Zebra's Song
(tune: L'il Liza Jane)

Zelda Zebra likes to zoom.
  She zooms with zest.
Zelda Zebra zig zags too.
  She does her best.
Zelda Zebra makes one big Z.
Zelda Zebra zips right past me!

❷ Guided Practice

Listen for /z/ and compare and review /p/ and /l/. Display Alphafriends *Pippa Pig* and *Larry Lion* opposite *Zelda Zebra*. Review each character's sound.

Hold up the Picture Cards one at a time. Children signal "thumbs up" for pictures that start with Zelda Zebra's sound, /z/, and a child puts the card below Zelda's picture. For "thumbs down" words, children put cards below the correct Alphafriends.

Pictures: *zipper, peach, leaf, purse, zip, lemon, zigzag, log, pot.*

Tell children that they will sort more pictures in the **Phonics Center** today.

❸ Apply

Have children complete **Practice Book** pages 43–44 at small group time.

 Phonics Center

Materials Phonics Center materials for Theme 7, Week 2, Day 1 · · · · · · · · · · · · · · · ·

Display Day 1 Direction Chart. Children put *Zelda Zebra, Pippa Pig,* and *Larry Lion* (without letters) in separate sections of Workmat 3. Then they sort remaining pictures by initial sound: /z/, /p/, and /l/.

Practice Book page 43

Name

THEME 7: Wheels Go Around
Week Two
Phonemic Awareness: /z/

Children
• color all the pictures on pages 43 and 44 that start like *Zelda Zebra*
• cut and paste pictures for that sound in the boxes on page 44
• draw something else that starts with that sound

Home Connection Let's name all the things on the front and back that start like *Zelda Zebra.*

43

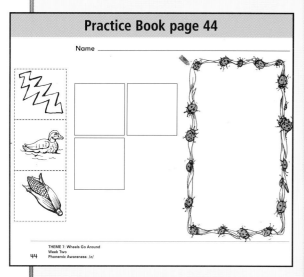

Practice Book page 44

Name

THEME 7: Wheels Go Around
Week Two
Phonemic Awareness: /z/

44

OBJECTIVES

- Read high-frequency words.
- Create and write sentences with high-frequency words.

Materials

- *Higglety Pigglety: A Book of Rhymes,* page 32
- **Word Cards** *and, I, like, my, see, to*
- **Picture Cards** *cat, dog, horse*
- **Punctuation Card** *period*

High-Frequency Words

Display and read the Word Cards *see, and, like, to, my,* and *I*.

- Call on children to identify each word and to match it on the Word Wall.

- Remind children that they will see these words often in books.

- Hold up **Word Cards** *to* and *see*. I'll read a poem. You listen for these two words.

- Read "Hey, Diddle, Diddle." Did you hear these words in the poem? Track the print as you reread the line with those words. Who will match the cards to the same words in this line?

- Repeat with *and*.

Higglety Pigglety: A Book of Rhymes, page 32

Have children write sentences.

- Add **Picture Cards** for *dog, cat,* and *horse* to the pocket chart.

- Begin a sentence with *I like,* and have children add cards to complete it.

- Encourage children to make up their own sentences to write. They can refer to the cards, use their knowledge of letter sounds to spell other words, and add drawings. Provide time for children to share their work.

ORAL LANGUAGE: VOCABULARY
Using Position Words

OBJECTIVES
● Use position words.

Materials
● **Read Aloud** *The Little Engine That Could*

❶ Teach

Display *The Little Engine That Could*.

● In *The Little Engine That Could,* where were the dolls, toys, and food? (on a train)

● Where were the cars holding the dolls, toys, and food? (behind the engine, on the tracks)

● Explain that words like *on* and *behind* tell where things are.

❷ Practice/Apply

Have children practice using position words.

● Work together to brainstorm a list of position words. List the words on a chart.

● Where am I standing? (beside the chart, in front of the group) Where is Janna sitting? (next to Gary, behind Wendy, on the floor)

● Move your marker to different places in the room, and have children tell where it is: under a chair, in the box, over the table.

● Review the chart, adding simple line drawings to help children "read" it.

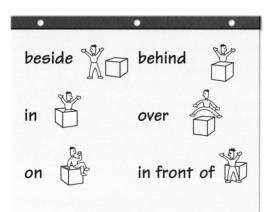

Writing Center

Put the chart in the Writing Center. Partners can review the pictures and talk about position words. Then have each child draw one favorite thing from *The Little Engine That Could* and write or dictate a label to describe its position.

English Language Learners

Choice of prepositions varies a great deal among languages. Expect interference from children's first language. Provide practice by placing items in various positions in relation to each other. Ask: *Where's the _____?* As children answer, assist them with vocabulary and usage as needed.

Day at a Glance
T90–T99

Learning to Read

Big Book, *T92*
Phonics: Initial Consonant *z, T94*
High Frequency Word: *have, T96*

Word Work

High-Frequency Word Practice, *T98*

Writing & Oral Language

Vocabulary Expansion, *T99*

Daily Routines

first   last

Sunday	Monday	Tuesday	Wednesday	Thursday	Friday	Saturday
			1	2	3	4
5	6	7	8	9	10	11
12	13	14	15	16	17	18
19	20	21	22	23	24	25
26	27	28	29	30	31	

Calendar

Reading the Calendar Extend yesterday's discussion of position words to your calendar routine. Who will show us the name of the day that is first every week? Which day is last? What is today's date? What number do you see before (after) it?

Daily Message

Modeled Writing
As you write today's news, pause to point out any words that tell where (position words). Have children tell why those words are helpful.

Today Marita will put food <u>in</u> Hammie's cage. Mark will put olive oil <u>on</u> Hammie's wheel.

Word Wall

High-Frequency Words Have partners read and spell words on the Word Wall today. Each partner can name five words for the other child to find and spell.

to	and	here

my	see

Word Cards for these words appear on pages R8–R10.

Daily Phonemic Awareness

Blending and Segmenting Phonemes

- Say: I will be the Little Engine that Could, and you can be the toys. When you knock, I'll ask a question. If you know the answer, I will let you on the train.

- Have children "knock" on a table or the floor. Ask: What is my code word? The sounds are /z/ . . . /ĭ/ . . . /p/.

- Have partners confer and raise their hands when they know the word. When most hands are up, have children say the word and then you say "All aboard!".

- Continue with *track, seat,* and *go.* Then change the game so that you say the whole word and partners count and say the separate sounds.

Getting Ready to Learn

To help children plan their day, tell them that they will–

- listen to a **Big Book:** *Vroom, Chugga, Vroom-Vroom.*

- learn the new letters *Z* and *z,* and look for words that begin with *z.*

- compare how far toy cars travel on a ramp in the Science Center.

OBJECTIVES

- Introduce concepts of print.
- Develop story language.
- Reinforce comprehension strategy and comprehension skill.

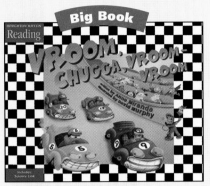

Big Book

Vroom, Chugga, Vroom-Vroom

Selection Summary Fast-paced, rhyming text describes the adventures of animal characters who compete in a great auto race.

Key Concepts

Races and contests

Parts of a car

Reading the Big Book

Building Background

Share the **Big Book's** title and by-line. Then preview the book. Explain that the story is make-believe but that it shows many things found in real car races.

Ask children who have seen a real car race on TV to tell how it was like the one pictured. Discuss how the helmets, the numerals on the cars, and the starting flag are used.

COMPREHENSION STRATEGY
Monitor/Clarify

Teacher Modeling Model how to clarify anything confusing in a story.

 Think Aloud If I've never been to a real car race, I may read things I don't understand. If I am confused by something, I can go back and read again. I can also look at the pictures for help. If I am still confused, I can ask someone to explain that part.

COMPREHENSION SKILL
Cause and Effect

Teacher Modeling Remind children that if they think about why things happen in a story, they will understand it better and enjoy it more.

Think Aloud Sometimes one thing happens and causes something else to happen. On the cover I see the crowd cheering and small clouds coming from the cars. I think the artist wanted me to figure out that the cars were going really fast. That's what caused those other things. As we read, let's think about why things happen.

Big Book Read Aloud

Read the selection, emphasizing the rhyme. Pause occasionally to let children contribute car numbers or rhyming words.

Responding

Oral Language: Personal Response Encourage children to use the language of the story as they react to it.

- What did you like best about the story?
- What did you learn about cars that you didn't know before? about car races?
- What was your favorite car in the race? Why?

Science Center

Materials sheet of cardboard • toy cars • blocks

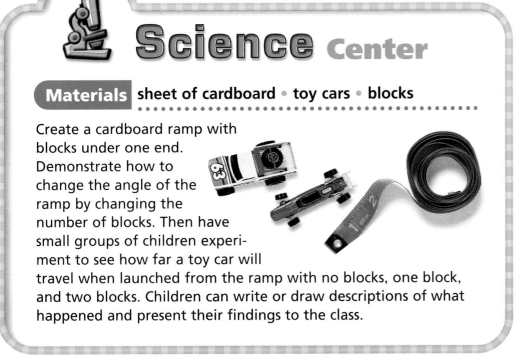

Create a cardboard ramp with blocks under one end. Demonstrate how to change the angle of the ramp by changing the number of blocks. Then have small groups of children experiment to see how far a toy car will travel when launched from the ramp with no blocks, one block, and two blocks. Children can write or draw descriptions of what happened and present their findings to the class.

REACHING ALL LEARNERS
Extra Support/ Intervention

Reinforce position words by pointing to various cars in the story and having a child describe where they are.

OBJECTIVES

- Identify words that begin with /z/.
- Identify pictures whose names begin with z.
- Form the letters Z, z.

Materials

- **Alphafriend Card** *Zelda Zebra*
- **Letter Cards** *l, p, z*
- **Picture Cards** for *z, p,* and *l*
- **Blackline Master** 182
- **Phonics Center** Theme 7, Week 2, Day 2

Zelda Zebra's Song

(tune: L'il Liza Jane)

Zelda Zebra likes to zoom.
 She zooms with zest.

Zelda Zebra zig zags too.
 She does her best.

Zelda Zebra makes one big Z.

Zelda Zebra zips right past me!

 PHONICS
Initial Consonant *z*

❶ Phonemic Awareness Warm-Up

Beginning Sound Read or sing the lyrics to Zelda Zebra's song and have children echo it line-for-line. Have them listen for the /z/ words and signal "thumbs up" for each one they hear. See Theme Resources page R3 for music and lyrics.

❷ Teach Phonics

Beginning Letter Display the *Zelda Zebra* card, and have children name the letter. The letter *z* stands for the sound /z/, as in *zebra*. When you see a *z*, remember Zelda Zebra. That will help you remember the sound /z/.

Write *zebra* on the board. Underline the *z*. This is the word *zebra*. What is the first letter in the word? (z) *Zebra* starts with /z/, so *z* is the first letter I write for *zebra*.

❸ Guided Practice

Compare and Review: *p, l* In a pocket chart, display the **Letter Cards** as shown and the **Picture Cards** in random order. Review the sounds for *z, p,* and *l*. Have children take turns naming a picture, saying its beginning sound, and putting the card below the right letter. Tell children they will sort more pictures in the **Phonics Center** today.

Extra Support/ Intervention

To help children remember the sound for *z*, point out that the letter's name gives a clue to its sound: *z*, /z/.

Z

Penmanship Rhyme: Z

From the top, zip right
with a line.
Slant down
to the left, and zip right
one more time:
It's a Z, big Z, big Z!

Penmanship Rhyme: z

From the middle, zip
right with a line.
Slant down to the left,
and zip right one more time:
It's a z, a small z, small z!

Penmanship: Writing Z, z Tell children that now they'll learn to write the letters that stand for /z/: capital *Z* and small *z*. Write each letter as you recite the penmanship rhyme. Children can chant each rhyme as they "write" the letter in the air.

❹ Apply

Have children complete **Practice Book** page 45 at small group time. For additional penmanship practice assign **Blackline Master** 182. Penmanship practice for the continuous stroke style is available on **Blackline Master** 208.

Practice Book page 45

Phonics Center

Materials Phonics Center materials for Theme 7, Week 2, Day 2 ....

Display Day 2 Direction Chart. Children put *Zelda Zebra, Pippa Pig,* and *Larry Lion* (with letters) in separate sections of Workmat 3. Then they sort remaining pictures by initial letter/sound: *z, p,* and *l*.

OBJECTIVES

- Read and write the high-frequency word *have*.

Materials

- **Word Cards** *A, a, have, I*
- **Picture Cards** *dog, farm, feet, pig*
- **Punctuation Card** *period*
- ***Higglety Pigglety: A Book of Rhymes,*** page 20
- **Teacher-made word cards** *big, can, 2*

INSTRUCTION

HIGH-FREQUENCY WORD
New Word: *have*

❶ Teach

Introduce the word *have*. Tell children that today they will learn to read and write a word that they will often see in stories. Say *have* and use it in context.

I *have* a bike.   I *have* to go home.   I *have* two dolls.

- Invite children to use the word *have* in oral sentences.

- Write *have* on the board, and ask children to spell it as you point to the letters. Say: Spell *have* with me, *h-a-v-e, have.*

- Lead a chant, clapping on each beat, to help children remember the spelling: *h-a-v-e, have! h-a-v-e, have!*

Word Wall Post *have* on the Word Wall, and remind children to look there when they need to remember how to write the word.

❷ Guided Practice

Build these sentences one at a time. Ask children to take turns reading the sentences.

Place the pocket chart in the Writing Center for children to build more sentences.

Notice

I have a dog,
I had a cat.
I've got a frog
Inside my hat.

by David McCord

20

Higglety Pigglety: A Book of Rhymes, page 20

Display *Higglety Pigglety: A Book of Rhymes,* page 20.

- Share the rhyme "Notice."

- Reread the poem, tracking the print and asking children to listen for the word *have.* Then recite the first line and ask a child to point to *have.*

❸ Apply

- Have children complete **Practice Book** page 46 at small group time.

- On Day 3 they will practice reading *have* in the **Phonics Library** story "Tan Van."

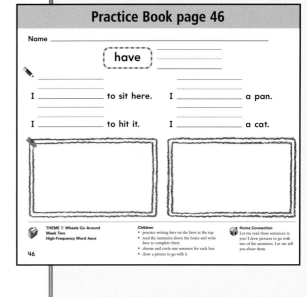

Practice Book page 46

Name _____

[have] _____

✏ _____

I _____ to sit here.   I _____ a pan.

I _____ to hit it.   I _____ a cat.

THEME 7: Wheels Go Around
Week Two
High-Frequency Word *have*

Children
• practice writing *have* on the lines at the top
• read the sentences above the boxes and write *have* to complete them
• choose and circle one sentence for each box
• draw a picture to go with it

Home Connection
Let me read these sentences to you! I drew pictures to go with two of the sentences. Let me tell you about them.

46

Monitoring Student Progress

If . . .	Then . . .
children have problems reading or writing *have* on the **Practice Book** page,	have them form the word with alphabet blocks or felt letters and use it in oral sentences.

PRACTICE

OBJECTIVES

- Read high-frequency words.
- Create and write sentences with high-frequency words.

Materials

- **Word Cards** *a, go, have, I, My*
- **Picture Cards** *bike, jeep*
- **Punctuation Card** *period*
- **Teacher-made word cards** *big, can*

High-Frequency Words

Build sentences about things with wheels.

- Display the **Word Cards** and **Picture Cards** in random order. Then put the **Word Card** for *I* in the pocket chart and read it.
- I want the next word to be *have.* Who can find that word? That's right! This word is *have.* Now who can read my sentence so far?
- Continue building the sentence *I have a big* _____. Have children choose a picture to complete it.
- Read the sentence together. Then continue with a new one.

Have children write sentences.

- Have each child write a sentence, using one from the pocket chart as a model.
- Children can choose a vehicle and add their own drawings. If children choose to write a different sentence, remind them to use what they know about letter sounds to help them spell the words.

VOCABULARY EXPANSION
Position Words, Parts of a Car

Listening/Speaking/Viewing

Review position words.
- Briefly review yesterday's work with words that tell where.
- Page through *Vroom, Chugga, Vroom-Vroom* together and ask children to describe where some of the cars are in each scene.

Discuss the position of car parts.
- Explain that position words can also tell where parts of a car are.
- Duplicate the car on **Blackline Master 106** and tape it to the center of a sheet of chart paper. Point to parts of the car and help children name them; add a label for each part.
- Duplicate and cut out the pictures of the auto parts on **Blackline Master 107.** Children can match them to the same parts on the diagram and use position words to tell where each part of the car is.

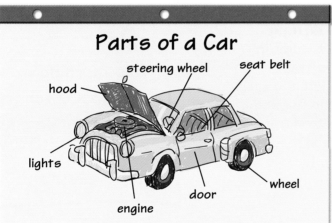

Parts of a Car

steering wheel · seat belt · hood · lights · engine · door · wheel

Dramatic Play Center

Materials blocks · toy cars and trucks

Have groups of children use blocks to outline "bays" in a "garage." Children can take turns "driving" small toy cars pulling into the garage, working on them, and backing them out. Encourage conversations about the cars' positions and features.

OBJECTIVES
- Name parts of a car.
- Use position words to describe parts of a car.

Materials
- **Big Book** *Vroom, Chugga, Vroom-Vroom*
- **Blackline Masters** 106–107

Vocabulary Support

The Vocabulary Reader can be used to develop and reinforce vocabulary related to the instruction for this week.

Vocabulary Reader

Vocabulary Readers

Let's Go!

by Sarah Curran

English Language Learners

Most English language learners will not know the parts of a car. Encourage these children to repeat the words English speakers name. Check for correct pronunciation of all the vowel sounds.

Day at a Glance
T100–T115

Learning to Read

Big Book, *T102*
Phonics: Reviewing Consonant *z;*
Short *i* Words, *T110*

Word Work

Building Words, *T114*

Writing & Oral Language

Shared Writing, *T115*

Daily Routines

Sunday	Monday	Tuesday	Wednesday	Thursday	Friday	Saturday
			1	2	3	4
5	6	7	8	9	10	11
12	13	14	15	16	17	18
19	20	21	22	23	24	25
26	27	28	29	30		

Calendar

Reading the Calendar To add variety to your calendar routine, suggest a "race" between sunny, cloudy, rainy, and snowy days. For the remainder of the month, children can write each day's date and draw a weather symbol. At month's end they can see which weather "wins."

Daily Message

Modeled Writing
Try to use *z* words in the daily message. Then call on children to circle each *z*. Help children see that letters stand for sounds in the beginning, the middle, and the end of a word.

This morning was ha(z)y and cool. (Z)achary (z)ipped up his coat. Katie wore a fu(zz)y sweater.

Word Wall

High-Frequency Words Choose a child to point to and read the new word that was added to the Word Wall this week, *have*. Children can compare *have* to other words on the Word Wall. *(Have has four letters like here and like; begins with /h/ like here; ends with an e like see, here.)*

have	like	here

Word Cards for these words appear on pages R8–R10.

Daily Phonemic Awareness

Blending and Segmenting Phonemes

Tell children that you will say some sounds and they should put them together to make a word that names part of a car.

- Pronounce /s/ /ē/ /t/, have children repeat the sounds with you, and then have someone say the word. (seat)

- Continue with these sounds: /h/ /ŏo/ /d/ (hood); /wh/ /ē/ /l/ (wheel); /l/ /ī/ /t/ (light).

- Now say these whole words, asking partners to say the separate sounds and count them: *belt, road, race.*

To help children plan their day, tell them that they will–

- reread and talk about the **Big Book** *Vroom, Chugga, Vroom-Vroom.*

- read a story called "Tan Van."

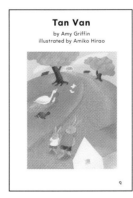

Tan Van
by Amy Griffin
illustrated by Amiko Hirao

9

- read, write, and explore more about wheels in the Centers.

Reading the Big Book

Reading for Understanding

Reread the story, emphasizing the rhythm and rhyme. Pause for discussion points.

COMPREHENSION SKILL

Cause and Effect

page 1

Teacher-Student Modeling Review that good readers think about what happens in a story and why. Prompts:

- The animals are hurrying. Can you tell why? (The race will start soon.)

Oral Language

On a rereading, point out the words that name or mimic sounds:
vroom, chugga, vroom-vroom the sound of the racing cars' engines
boom the sound of hearts pounding
zoom the sound of speed

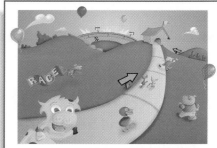

Vroom, chugga, vroom-vroom.
Race is going to start soon!

1

Banners wave.
Fans cheer!

2

Cars are checked.
The start's near.

3

1 is at the starting gate.
2 and 3 can hardly wait.

4

4 and 5 check brakes and lights.
6 makes sure his seatbelt's tight.

5

7's in the pole position.
8 and 9 start their ignitions.

10 and 11 zip up suits.
12 and 13 put on boots.

6 **7**

14, 15 call their crews.
16 tightens two loose screws.

17, 18 rev in place.
19 wants to set the pace.

8 **9**

20 lines up last in row.
Green lights flash.
Get ready, GO!

Vroom, chugga, VROOM-VROOM!
Hearts pound, BOOM, BOOM!
Flag waves and ZOOM, ZOOM!

10 **11**

TARGET SKILL

COMPREHENSION STRATEGY
Monitor/Clarify

pages 6–7

Teacher-Student Modeling Remind children that if they do not understand something, the pictures can help. Prompts:

- How does the picture help explain what "start their ignitions" means? (Exhaust shows the cars are running; the ignition must start a car's engine.)

CRITICAL THINKING
Guiding Comprehension

pages 8–9

- **DRAWING CONCLUSIONS** Why do 14 and 15 call their crews? (14 has a flat; 15 is sick.) What does a crew do? (take care of cars)

TARGET SKILL

REVISITING THE TEXT
Concepts of Print

pages 10–11

Matching words; Using all capitals
- Frame *go* on page 10 and have children spell it; do the same with *go* on the Word Wall. A word is always spelled the same.

- Words spelled with all capital letters show excitement. Frame *Go* in the art on pages 10 and 11; have children spell it and then say it as the starter would.

CRITICAL THINKING
Guiding Comprehension

pages 12–13

- **DRAWING CONCLUSIONS** What is made of rubber on a car? (tires, wheels) How does the picture show that the tires are burning, or losing rubber? (by the marks on the road)

pages 14–15

- **NOTING DETAILS** What job do you think the bird on page 14 has? How do you know that? (race announcer; has a microphone)

COMPREHENSION STRATEGY
Monitor/Clarify

pages 16–17

Teacher-Student Modeling What does it mean to blow a tire? How does the picture show this?

- What is the pit? (an area off the track where cars are fixed)

- What could you do if the picture and rereading didn't help you understand what a pit is? (ask someone for help)

Rubber, rubber, burn, burn . . .

12

Racers take the first turn.

13

12   **13**

Down the straight they flash like lightning.
Hold your breath. It's so exciting!

14

Speeding madly 'round the curve,
Number 3 begins to swerve.

15

14   **15**

16's blown his left rear tire.
7's engine has caught on fire!

16

12 and 13 have to quit.
17 is in the pit.

17

16   **17**

19 just ran out of gas.
11's blocked and cannot pass.

18

4 is stuck in second gear.
Number 6 brings up the rear.

19

18　　　　　　　　　　　　　**19**

8 just made a big mistake.
18 has to hit the brake.

20

10 and 20 brush the wall.
15's muffler's going to fall.

21

20　　　　　　　　　　　　　**21**

2 and 5 are nose to nose.
14's steering wheel just froze.

22

1 is spinning off the track.
Several cars are falling back.

23

22　　　　　　　　　　　　　**23**

TARGET SKILL

COMPREHENSION SKILL
Cause and Effect

pages 18–21

Student Modeling What happens to car 11 (page 18)? Why can't it pass? (It's blocked.) What does car 18 do (page 20)? Why does it have to hit its brakes? (to avoid hitting the bugs crossing the track)

CRITICAL THINKING
Guiding Comprehension

pages 22–23

- **MAKING JUDGMENTS** Why do you think most of the cars in the story are having trouble? (They are driving too fast.) Away from the race track, real drivers have speed limits and other traffic rules to follow. Why?

REACHING ALL LEARNERS

Challenge

Children who can easily match words in the text may be able to find and read words from the Word Wall. At small group time, give these children a list of things to find in the story.

CRITICAL THINKING
Guiding Comprehension

pages 24–25

- **MAKING INFERENCES** Which car is ahead on page 24? Which car do you think will win the race? (number 9) What does a car have to do to win a race? (cross the finish line)

page 26

- **CHARACTERS** How do you think the driver feels about winning the race? How do you know?

page 27

- **MAKING INFERENCES** What do you think will happen next? Why? (Another race will start; cars are lining up.)

COMPREHENSION STRATEGY
Monitor/Clarify

page 29

STUDENT MODELING What can you do to figure out what the word *test* means here? (look at the picture, read on) What does *test* mean in this story? (a contest, a race)

Vroom, chugga, vroom-vroom!
Someone's going to win soon!

24

Which car's first across the line?
Hurrah! It's driver number 9!

25

24   **25**

9 has won a golden cup.

26

But look! More cars are lining up.

27

26   **27**

There's going to be another race.

28

Another test. Another chase.

29

28   **29**

English Language Learners

Revisit the text with a small group and let children tell you what is happening in each picture. After discussing each page, read the text to confirm or clarify children's explanations.

T106   **THEME 7: Wheels Go Around**

Vroom, chugga, vroom-vroom.
Start your engine! ZOOM-ZOOM!

30

30

CRITICAL THINKING

Guiding Comprehension

page 30

- **MAKING JUDGMENTS** How do the fans feel about the start of a new race? How does the driver feel? Do you think you would like to see a car race? Why or why not?

COMPREHENSION SKILL

Cause and Effect

Student Modeling Have children browse through the book to find examples of something that happened and what caused it. Children can tell in their own words what happened in the picture and why.

 English Language Learners

Tell children you will read the story again, pausing whenever they want you to talk about something. Encourage all children to raise their hands when they want to stop and hear more about what something means.

Reading the Big Book **T107**

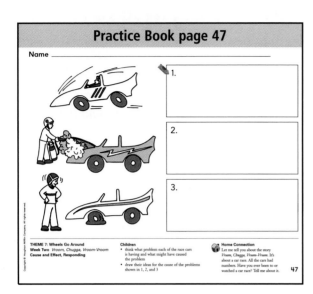

Responding

Oral Language: Retelling

Use these prompts to help children retell the story:

- Where does this story take place? What is it about?
- What kinds of problems did some of the cars have? What caused the problems?
- Which car won the race?
- What did you like best about the story?

Oral Language: Literature Circle Have small groups compare the cars in this story to real ones. What parts of this story are like things in real life? What makes this story make-believe?

Practice Book Children will complete **Practice Book** page 47 during small group time.

Monitoring Student Progress

If . . .	Then . . .
children need more practice identifying cause-effect relationships,	review some familiar stories and help children tell what happens and why.

Art Center

Materials construction paper rectangles, squares, circles • glue ·····································

Cut out rectangles, squares, and circles of various colors and sizes and place them in the Art Center. Children can arrange the shapes on paper to design cars, glue them in place, and add details with crayons or markers.

Math Center

Materials *Wheels Around* • *Vroom, Chugga, Vroom-Vroom* • counters • self-stick notes ···················

Introduce the activity by displaying a side-view picture of a car in either book. Point out that although only two wheels are shown, two more appear on the other side of the car. Put down two counters for the two visible wheels, then two more for the ones that can't be seen. Don't forget to add one for the steering wheel! Count the markers, write *5* on the self-stick note, and post it at the edge of the page. At group time, children can follow your example to find out how many wheels the different vehicles in *Wheels Around* have.

- Identify words with initial consonant *z*, /z/.
- Blend and read words with *b, d, f, p, r, z*, and short *i*.

Materials

- **Alphafriend Cards** *Iggy Iguana, Zelda Zebra*
- **Letter Cards** *a, b, d, f, g, i, l, n, p, r, t, z*
- **Alphafriend CD** Theme 7
- **Blending Routines Card 1**

Practice Book page 48

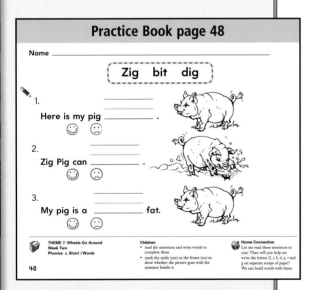

Name _____

Zig   bit   dig

1. _____
Here is my pig _____ .
☺ ☹

2. _____
Zig Pig can _____ .
☺ ☹

3. _____
My pig is a _____ fat.
☺ ☹

THEME 7: Wheels Go Around
Week Two
Phonics: z; Short *i* Words

Children
• read the sentences and write words to complete them
• mark the smile (yes) or the frown (no) to show whether the picture goes with the sentence beside it.

Home Connection
Let me read these sentences to you! Then will you help me write the letters *Z, i, b, d, p, r* and *g* on separate scraps of paper? We can build words with them.

48

Monitoring Student Progress

If . . .	Then . . .
children have trouble blending words such as *rig* or *big*,	repeat this lesson using **Blending Routines Card 2,** *Sound-by Sound Blending*.

PHONICS

Blending Short *i* Words

❶ Teach: Connect Sounds to Letters

Review consonant *z*. Ask children what letter and sound they think of when they see Zelda Zebra.

- Play Zelda Zebra's song, and have children clap for each /z/ word.
- Write *Z* and *z* on the board, and list words from the song.

Review short *i*. Tell children that they'll build a word with *d*, but first they'll need a vowel ("helper letter").

- Display Alphafriend *Iggy Iguana*. Iggy Iguana will help us build words today. Iggy's letter is the vowel *i*, and one sound *i* stands for is /ĭ/.
- Hold up the **Letter Card** *i*. Say /ĭ/. Listen for /ĭ/ in these words: /ĭ/ *if*, /ĭ/ *inch*, /ĭ/ *igloo*.

Model Blending Routine 1. Now show the **Letter Cards** *d, i,* and *g*. Have children identify each letter and the sound it stands for.

- Review blending the sounds as you point to each letter with a sweeping motion. I say the sounds in order: first /d/, then /ĭ/, then /g/. I hold each sound until I say the next one, *dĭĭg, dig*. Repeat, having children blend and pronounce *dig* with you.
- Show **Letter Cards** *z, i,* and *g*. Model blending the sounds as you point to the letters with a sweeping motion: *zzzĭĭg, zig*.
- Repeat, having children blend the word on their own. Tell children that *zig* means to move to the side quickly.

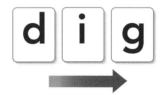   

❷ Guided Practice

Check Understanding. Display words *bit, lap,* and *fan* and have children blend each word. Then display *pin, tab,* and *fin*. Have children blend the words, modeling blending as needed. Display the sentence *I have a pig*. Children should recognize the underlined words from the Word Wall. Tell them to blend the other word to read the sentence.

❸ Apply

Children complete **Practice Book** page 48 at small group time.

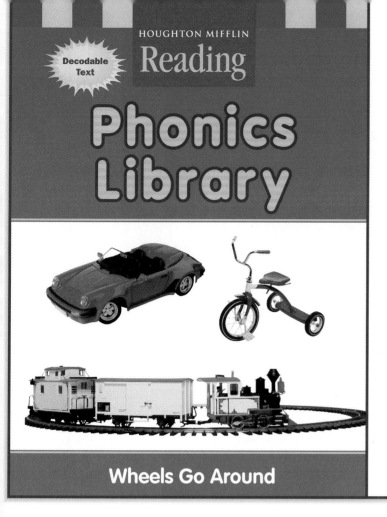

Wheels Go Around

Tan Van

by Amy Griffin
illustrated by Amiko Hirao

9

PHONICS LIBRARY

Reading Decodable Text

Phonics/Decoding Strategy

Teacher-Student Modeling Discuss using the Phonics/Decoding strategy to read words in the story.

Think Aloud Let's read the title. The first word begins with capital *T*. The sound for *T* is /t/. The next letters are *a* and *n*. I blend the letters to read this word: *tă ăn, tan.* The next word begins with capital *V*. It also has an *a* and an *n*. Let's blend the sounds to read this word, *vvvă ăn, van.* Do you see a van coming down the road? I wonder what kind of van it is.

Preview the pictures on pages 10–11. Write *Zig Pig* on the board and explain that it is the name of one of the characters in the story. Model blending the word *Zig* for children. Have individuals read *Pig* and model how they blended it.

It is a tan van!

10

Zig Pig ran.
Can I have it?

11

Prompts for Decoding

Have children read each page silently before reading aloud to you. Remind children to look at each letter as they sound out the word. Prompts:

page 10 What kind of van is it? (ice-cream van)

page 11 What word rhymes with *Zig* on this page? What letters are the same in these words?

page 12 Read the word that tells what Dan Cat did. (ran) Why did he do that? (He wanted to get to the van before it left.) Have a child model blending the word *ran*.

Word Key

Decodable words with short *i* and short *a* —————

High-Frequency Words ————

Dan Cat ran.
Can I have it?

12

Zig Pig sat.
Dan Cat sat.

13

Oral Language

Discuss the story. Remind children to speak in complete sentences.

- How do you think Zig Pig and Dan Cat felt when they saw the van? (They were happy and excited.)
- Do you think the driver of the tan van likes her job? Why? (She likes her job. It makes the animals happy.)
- What are some words that might describe how the ice cream tastes? (cool, good, sweet)

Identify rhyming words. Ask children to reread the story and identify rhyming words. *(pig, Zig; tan, van, ran, can, Dan; cat, sat)* Have children model blending the words. Remind them to hold each sound until they say the next one.

 ## Build Fluency

Model fluent reading.

- Read aloud page 11. Then have children read the page aloud.
- Have children reread the same page several times until each child can read it aloud smoothly.

 Home Connection
Have children color the pictures in the take-home version of "Tan Van." After rereading on Day 4, they can read it to family members at home. (See **Phonics Library Blackline Masters**.)

REACHING ALL LEARNERS

Extra Support/Intervention

Reread "Zebra" on page 3 of **Higglety Pigglety**. Have children give "thumbs up" for each /z/ word they hear. Have children frame *z* words for you to read; ask them what sound *z* stands for in those words.

Reading Decodable Text **T113**

OBJECTIVES

- Blend consonant sounds with short *i* to read words.

Materials

- Letter Cards *a, b, D, d, f, g, i, k, m, n, p, r, t, z*

BUILDING WORDS
Words with Short *i*

Model building the word *dig*.

- Display **Letter Cards** *a, b, D, d, f, g, i, k, m, n, p, r, t,* and *z*.

- Model how to build the word *dig* with **Letter Cards.** Listen as I stretch out the sounds: /d//ĭ//g/. How many sounds do you hear? The first sound is /d/. I'll put up a *d* to spell that. The next sound is /ĭ/. What letter should I choose for that? The last sound is /g/. What letter spells /g/? Blend /d/, /ĭ/, and /g/ and read *dĭĭĭg, dig*.

Model building words that rhyme with *dig*.

- Tell children you want to build a word that rhymes with *dig*.

- Replace *d* with *f* and say: Now what happens if I change /d/ to /f/?

- Continue making and blending short *i* words by substituting *b, r, p,* and *z*.

Word Wall Have a volunteer find *dig* on the Word Wall. Remind children that they can use *dig* to help them read and write words that rhyme with *dig*.

Check Understanding Have small groups work together to build the word *rig*. They can use letter tiles or other manipulative letters in your collection. Provide corrections as needed. Have children build other short *i* words.

Extend Practice Ask children to build these words: *mad, Dan, pit, ham, kit, man*. Display the sentence <u>I see a</u> big pig. Have children read the sentence, blending the sounds for *big* and *pig*. (Underlined words are from the Word Wall.)

SHARED WRITING
Writing a Class Story

DAY
3

OBJECTIVES
- Plan a beginning for a class story.

Materials
- **Big Book** *Vroom, Chugga, Vroom-Vroom*

WRITING

WEEK 2

Review story structure.

- Remind children that stories usually have three important parts: a beginning, a middle, and an end.

- Explain that we often read about the characters' problem at the beginning of a story.

- Reread a few pages of *Vroom, Chugga, Vroom-Vroom*. Ask what the racers did at the beginning and what their problem was. (They were getting ready to race and all wanted to win.)

Invite children to help you write a class story.

- Ask children what kind of vehicle would they like to write about. List children's suggestions on chart paper. Then have them vote on one type.

- Ask: What problems might the vehicle have in the beginning? Help children brainstorm ideas. List them on a chart, and have the class vote for one.

- Incorporate children's suggestions in a shared writing experience.

- After introducing the character and its problem, tell children that tomorrow they will help you write about what happens next and think of a good solution.

Little Tow Truck

No one wanted

Little Tow Truck.

He was too little to help

other trucks.

Day at a Glance
T116–T123

Learning to Read

Big Book, *T118*
Phonics: Reviewing Consonant *z*; Blending Short *i* Words, *T120*

Word Work

Building Words, *T122*

Writing & Oral Language

Interactive Writing, *T123*

Daily Routines

Sunday	Monday	Tuesday	Wednesday	Thursday	Friday	Saturday
			1	2	3	4
5	6	7	8	9	10	11
12	13	14	15	16	17	18
19	20	21	22	23	24	25
26	27	28	29	30	31	

Calendar

Reading the Calendar Talk about the positions of numbers on the calendar. What number comes *before* 11? What number comes *after* 11? Find 15. What two numbers is it *between?* What number is *above* 15? below?

Daily Message

Modeled Writing
Use words more than once in the daily message. Then call on children to find and match words that are the same.

Yesterday <u>we</u> had a (book) about make-believe race cars. Today <u>we</u> will read a (book) about real vehicles.

Word Wall

High-Frequency Words Distribute cards for the words on the Word Wall. Have children take turns matching their cards to the same words on the Word Wall. Ask the class to chant each spelling: *h-a-v-e* spells *have; a-n-d* spells *and.*

have	and	here

Word Cards for these words appear on pages R8–R10.

Daily Phonemic Awareness

Blending and Segmenting Phonemes

Play a guessing game. Display the backs of the **Picture Cards** for *dog, mat, cat, desk,* and *lamp.* Tell children they'll blend sounds to guess the pictures.

- Listen and blend these sounds: /k/ . . . /ă/ . . . /t/. What do you get? (cat) Display **Picture Card** *cat.* Continue with the other pictures.

- This time I'll name a picture. You say its sounds like this: cat . . . /k/ /ă/ /t/. Now you try it. Continue with the other **Picture Cards,** asking children to segment and count the sounds.

Getting Ready to Learn

To help children plan their day, tell them that they will–

- read the Science Link: *Cool Wheels!*

- learn to make and read new words.

- read a book called "Tan Van."

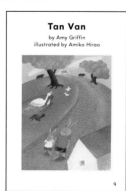

OBJECTIVES

- Identify cause and effect relationships.
- Match words in print.

Big Book

Cool Wheels!

Science Link

Oral Language

scooter A scooter is a motor bike—a bike with a motor. A scooter is like a motorcycle but smaller.

 Challenge

Prepare cards for the words and end marks in one or two sentences from the selection. One child builds a sentence and then challenges a partner to read it and find it in the book.

English Language Learners

Ask children if they have ever heard the word *cool.* Ask, *What do you think* cool *means?* Tell them that it has several meanings. It can mean *chilly,* or *cold,* but in this article it means *special.*

INSTRUCTION

READING THE BIG BOOK
Science Link

Building Background

Display the title page for *Cool Wheels!* and read it aloud. Have you ever seen wheels like these? What do these wheels look like? (skateboard with wagon wheels) What do you think "cool" means? Invite children to tell about other wheels they think are "cool."

Reading for Understanding Pause for discussion as you share the selection.

 COMPREHENSION STRATEGY
Monitor/Clarify

page 33
Student Modeling Is there anything about the title or this picture that confuses you? If so, what could you do to understand it better? (look at the pictures; reread or read on; ask for help)

 COMPREHENSION SKILL
Cause and Effect

pages 34–35
Student Modeling Remind children that sometimes one thing causes another thing to happen. Ask: What makes a skateboard and a skate go? (Person uses leg power to push off and move the wheels; going downhill causes wheels to roll on their own.)

A skateboard has wheels.
What makes it go?

34

A skate has wheels.
What makes it go?

35

34   35

A bike has wheels.
What makes it go?

36

A wheelchair has wheels.
What makes it go?

37

36   37

A scooter has wheels.
What makes it go?

38

Do you have some cool wheels?
What makes them go?

39

38   39

Guiding Comprehension

pages 36–37

- **COMPARE AND CONTRAST** How is what makes a bike go different from what makes a wheelchair go? What is the same? How is this wheelchair different from wheelchairs you have seen?

page 38

- **DRAWING CONCLUSIONS** Why is it important to wear helmets and other safety equipment when riding these cool wheels?

page 39

- **MAKING JUDGMENTS** Have you seen some cool wheels? What makes them special?

TARGET SKILL REVISITING THE TEXT

Concepts of Print

pages 34–35

Match Words in Print

- Read aloud page 34. Frame the word *has* and identify it. Call on children to find the same word on page 35. How do you know the words are the same?

- Continue with other words that are repeated on the two pages: *A, wheels, What, makes, it, go.*

Responding

Oral Language: Summarizing Point out that the author thinks many wheels are special, and ask children to name them. Which wheels did they like best? Why?

OBJECTIVES

- Identify initial *z* for words that begin with /z/.
- Blend and read words with initial consonants with short *i*.

Materials

- *From Apples to Zebras: A Book of ABC's,* page 27
- **Alphafriend Card** *Iggy Iguana*
- **Letter Cards** *a, b, d, f, g, h, i, k, n, p, r, t, z*
- **Picture Card** *dog*
- **Punctuation Cards** period, question mark
- **Phonics Center** Theme 7, Week 2, Day 4
- **Blending Routines Card 1**
- **Teacher-made word card** *can*

PHONICS
Blending Short *i* Words

Review consonant z. Using self-stick notes, cover the words on page 27 of *From Apples to Zebras: A Book of ABC's.* Then display the page. Ask what letter children expect to see first in each word and why. Uncover the words so children can check their predictions.

Review short i. Ask if children remember which Alphafriend stands for the vowel sound /ĭ/. Display Iggy Iguana and have children name other words that start with /ĭ/. *(into, igloo, itch, instrument)*

Zz

zebra

Zucchini

zucchini | zipper

27

From Apples to Zebras: A Book of ABC's, **page 27**

Review Blending Routine 1. Hold up **Letter Cards** *d, i,* and *g.* Now watch and listen as I build *dig:* /d/ /ĭ/ /g/, *dĭĭg, dig.*

- Replace the *d* with **Letter Card** *z.* Now let's blend my new word: /z/ /ĭ/ /g/, *zzzĭĭg, zig.*

 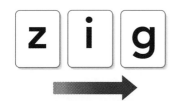

- Continue, choosing children to build and blend *big, fig,* and *rig.* Monitor responses to see who needs help blending.

Check Understanding Display the word *pig* and ask individuals to blend the word.

For more practice, display *Dan, pat,* and *pig.* Have children blend the words, modeling blending as needed. Remind children to hold each sound until they say the next one. Continue as children blend *fit, hat, Liz.* Then have children read the sentence <u>A</u> *pig* <u>is</u> <u>here</u>. Children should recognize the underlined words from the Word Wall. Tell them to blend the other word to read the sentence.

Practice/Apply In a pocket chart, build the sentence *Dog can dig.* with **Letter Cards** and **Picture Cards**.

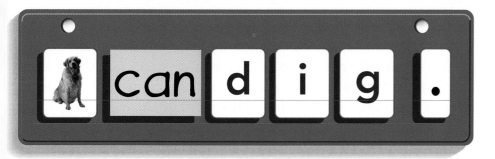

- Repeat the activity with *Can a <Picture Card: dog> dig?*
- Ask what letters you need to spell each sound in *big* and *pig*. Build the words with **Letter Cards**.
- Have children complete **Practice Book** page 49 at small group time.
- In groups today, children will also read short *i* words as they reread the **Phonics Library** story "Tan Van." See suggestions, pages T111–T113.

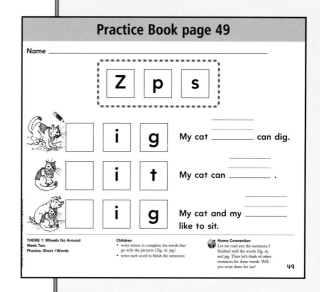

Practice Book page 49

Phonics Center

Materials Phonics Center materials for Theme 7, Week 2, Day 4 ·····················

Display Day 4 Direction Chart and Workmat 5. Children build short *i* words (*dig, pig, big*) with **Letter Cards**, sound by sound. Then they use **Word** and **Picture Cards** to build the sentence *I like my big pig.*

Monitoring Student Progress

If . . .	Then . . .
children have trouble building words and sentences,	have them work with you or a partner.
children can easily build words and sentences,	have them work with partners to build original sentences with short *i* words.

OBJECTIVES

- Blend consonant sounds with short *i* and short *a* to read words.

Materials

- **Letter Cards** *a, b, c, d, f, g, h, i, l, m, n, p, r, s, t, z*

PRACTICE

BUILDING WORDS
Words with Short *i* or Short *a*

Review building the word *dig*.

- Display **Letter Cards** *a, b, c, d, f, g, h, i, l, m, n, p, r, s, t,* and *z*.

- Review how to build *dig* in a pocket chart.

- Let's build *dig.* How many sounds do you hear? The first sound is /d/. I'll put up a *d* to spell that. The next sound is /ĭ/. What letter stands for that sound? I'll add the letter *i* to the chart. What is the last sound you hear? Add the letter *g* to the chart. Model blending the word, *dĭĭg, dig.*

- Choose children to build more short *i* words using *p, b, f, r,* and *z*.

Review building words with short *i* and short *a*.

- Listen: /ĭ/ /t/ ĭĭt, *it.* How many sounds do you hear? What letter spells the sound /ĭ/? The last sound is /t/. What letter spells that sound? Blend /ĭ/ and /t/ to read ĭĭĭt, *it.* Ask which letter you should add to build *lit.*

- Replace *l* with *p.* What happens if I change /l/ to /p/? Continue making and blending other words that rhyme with *lit* by substituting *f, h, s.*

- Repeat, this time building *at* and making new words by substituting initial consonants *b, c, f, h, m, p, r, s.*

Check Understanding Have children build some short *i* and short *a* words with magnetic letters. Ask them to first build *fig* and then *hat.* Provide corrections as necessary.

Extend Practice Invite children to build *pan, lap, hip,* and *fit.* Exaggerate the final sound in each word to help children name the correct final consonant. Display the sentence *I see a pig.* Have children read it, blending the sounds for the word *pig.* (Underlined words are from the Word Wall.)

Challenge

Children who can blend words with short *i* easily can build a personal word bank of short *i* words in their journals.

INTERACTIVE WRITING
Writing a Class Story

OBJECTIVES

● Continue a class story, dictating the middle and ending.
● Write letters or words for an interactive writing activity.

Build on the Shared Writing story.

● Together, reread the beginning of the story children helped to develop in yesterday's Shared Writing. (See page T115.)

● Review that the beginning of a story usually tells about the main character's problem. Have children name their story character and its problem.

● Next, have children brainstorm ways the problem might be solved. List ideas on a chart. Then have the class vote on one to write about.

● Have children dictate the story, one line at a time. As you write the story, skip lines on the chart paper to allow room for additions and changes.

● Occasionally, call on children to write initial or final consonants, spell high-frequency words, or help you build words.

● Reread the story together.

Writing Center

Post today's work in the Writing Center. Children can choose the beginning, middle, or end of the story, draw an illustration on art paper, and add a caption. Recopy the story onto sheets of drawing paper and bind them together with the illustrations to form a class book.

Day at a Glance
T124–T131

Learning to Read

Revisiting the Literature, *T126*
Phonics: Review Consonants;
Short *i* or *a* Words, *T128*

Word Work

Building Words, *T130*

Writing & Oral Language

Independent Writing, *T131*

Daily Routines

Sunday	Monday	Tuesday	Wednesday	Thursday	Friday	Saturday
			1	2	3	4
5	6	7	8	9	10	11
12	13	14	15	16	17	18
19	20	21	22	23	24	25
26	27	28	29	30	31	

Calendar

Reading the Calendar Have children compare this week's weather with last week's. How many days had sunny (rainy, snowy, overcast) weather last week? this week? Which week had more (fewer) days like that?

snowy day

rainy day

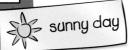

sunny day

Daily Message

Interactive Writing
Write about your plans for the weekend and invite children to share theirs. Have children spell or write their own names and supply familiar initial consonants for words.

Pat will visit her grandma.
Raul can help his dad wash the van.

Word Wall

High-Frequency Words Read the Word Wall together. Then play a rhyming game: I see a word on the Word Wall that rhymes with *fig.* The word is *dig.* Now raise your hand when you find a word that rhymes with *door.* (for)

dig   for

Word Cards for these words appear on pages R8–R10.

Daily Phonemic Awareness

Blending and Segmenting Phonemes

- Display "Stop and Go" on page 30 of *Higglety Pigglety*.

- Read the poem, stopping before *see*. I'll say the sounds, and you guess the word: /s/ /ē/. Say the sounds with me: /s/ /ē/. What word is it? (see) Who will show us what *see* means?

- Continue, segmenting *red* and *go*. Have children blend them.

- Now reverse the procedure. Say each whole word (*see*, *red* and *go*) slowly, and have children count and say its separate sounds.

Higglety Pigglety: A Book of Rhymes, page 30

To help children plan their day, tell them that they will–

- reread and talk about all the books they've shared this week.

- take home a story they can read.

- write in their journals.

OBJECTIVES

● Review the week's selections.

REVISITING THE LITERATURE
Literature Discussion

Review the week's selections, using these suggestions.

● Have volunteers tell what happened in the beginning, in the middle, and at the end of *The Little Engine That Could.*

● Page through *Vroom, Chugga, Vroom-Vroom,* and have children take turns telling what happened in the race.

● Have children tell what is special about *Cool Wheels!* as they discuss the photographs.

● On the board write *Zig Pig,* the name of a character in "Tan Van." Ask children how they blended the sounds to read the name.

● Ask children to vote for their favorite book of the week. Then read aloud the winner.

COMPREHENSION SKILL
Cause and Effect

Compare Books Remind children that in stories and in real life, one event can cause something to happen. Browse through each selection together, point out an appropriate event, and have children tell what caused it.

Rereading for Fluency

Reread Familiar Texts Remind children that they've learned the new word *have* and that they've learned to read short *i* words. As children reread the **Phonics Library** story "Tan Van," have them look for short *i* words.

- Feature several familiar **Phonics Library** titles in the Book Corner. Have children demonstrate their growing skills by choosing one to reread aloud.

- Children can alternate pages with a partner. From time to time, ask children to point out words or pages that they can read more easily now.

Oral Reading Frequent rereadings of familiar texts help children develop a more expressive style in their oral reading. Model how to read the questions in "Tan Van" as Zig Pig and Dan Cat might have said them. Then have children try it.

Tan Van
by Amy Griffin
illustrated by Amiko Hirao

Big Rig
by Amy Griffin
illustrated by Bob Kolar

Fan
by Amy Griffin
illustrated by Dagmar Fehlau

Assign Blackline Master 36. Children complete the page and take it home to share their reading progress. A copy appears on page R13.

My Reading Log

I can read

My new words

have   dig

Books for Small-Group Reading

The materials listed below provide reading practice for children at different levels.

Vocabulary Reader
Let's Go!

Leveled Reader

Going for a Ride

Little Big Book

Reading
VROOM, VROOM, CHUGGA VROOM

Little Readers for Guided Reading

Houghton Mifflin Classroom Bookshelf

Home Connection

Remind children to share the take-home version of "Tan Van" with their families.

OBJECTIVES

- Build and read words with initial consonants and short *a* or short *i*.
- Make sentences with high-frequency words.

Materials

- **Word Cards** *a, for, have, I my*
- **Picture Cards** *dog, leash*
- **Punctuation Card** period

PHONICS

Consonants, Short *a* or Short *i* Words

❶ Review

Review building words with short *i* and short *a*. Tell children that they will take turns being Word Builders and Word Readers. Have a group of Word Builders stand with you at the chalkboard.

- Let's build the word *dig*. First, count the sounds: /d/ /ĭ/ /g/. I know *d* stands for /d/, *i* stands for /ĭ/, and *g* stands for /g/. Let's write the letters.

- Replace *d* with *p*. The Word Builders do the same and ask the rest of the class (Word Readers) what new word was made.

- Have a new group of Word Builders come to the board. At your direction, they erase the *p*, write *b*, and ask the Word Readers to say the new word. Continue the activity with *zig* and *fig*.

- Now challenge children to show what letter they should replace to change *fig* to *fit*. Continue with *bit, pit, quit, sit, hit; hat, mat, fat; fan, Nan, van*.

dig pig

HIGH-FREQUENCY WORDS
I, see, my, like, a, to, and, go, for, have

❷ Review

Review the high-frequency words from the Word Wall.

- Have children echo-read the high-frequency words as you point to each one on the Word Wall.

- Then give each small group the **Word Cards, Picture Cards,** and **Punctuation Card** needed to make a sentence. Each child holds one card.

- Children stand and arrange themselves to make a sentence for others to read.

- After the class reads the sentence, have them act it out.

❸ Practice/Apply

- Children can complete **Practice Book** page 50 independently and read it to you during small group time.

- Have children take turns reading selections from the **Phonics Library** aloud to the class. Each child might read one page of "Tan Van," "Big Rig," or a favorite **Phonics Library** selection from the previous theme. Remind readers to share the pictures.

- Use questions for discussion like the following:

- Do you hear any rhyming words? What letters are the same in those words?

- Find a word that starts with the same sound as Zelda Zebra's name. What is the letter? What is the sound?

- This week we added the word *have* to the Word Wall. Find *have* in "Tan Van."

Practice Book page 50

Name _____

| have | for | is | Here |

1. I _____ a big fig.
2. Is it _____ Pig?
3. It _____ for Pig and Cat.
4. _____ is a big fig. A big fig

THEME 7: Wheels Go Around
Week Two
High-Frequency Words Review *have, for, is, here*
50

Children
- read the speech balloons
- write a word from the box to complete what the characters are saying
- color the pictures

Home Connection
Let me read this cartoon to you. Then maybe you can read a newspaper cartoon to me.

Monitoring Student Progress

If . . .	Then . . .
children need help remembering the consonant sounds,	show how these letters' names give clues to their sounds.
children pause at high-frequency words in **Phonics Library** selections,	have partners use flash cards to practice word recognition.

OBJECTIVES

- Blend consonants with short *a* and short *i* to read words.

Materials

- **Letter Cards** *a, b, c, D, f, g, h, i, l, m, n, p, q, u, r, s, t, v, z*

BUILDING WORDS
Words with Short *a* and Short *i*

Build words that rhyme with *it*.

- Use **Letter Cards** to build *it* in a pocket chart. Remind children to hold each sound as they say the next one, ĭ ĭ ĭt.

- Along the bottom of the pocket chart, line up the letters *b, f, h, l, p, q, u,* and *s.* I want to build the word *lit, lĭ ĭ ĭt.* Who can tell me which letter I should take from here to make *lit?*

- Have a volunteer take the letter *l* and place it in front of *it.* Continue building short *i* words, using initial consonants *b, f, h, p, q,* and *s.*

- On chart paper, keep a list of all the words you make, and reread the list together.

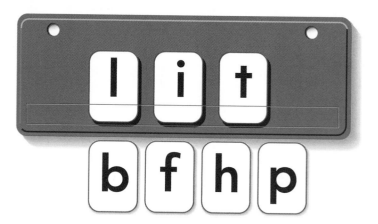

Build words with short *i* and short *a.*

- Continue building short *i* and short *a* words. Examples: *can, Dan, fan, man; bat, cat, pat, rat, vat; big, pig, rig, zig.*

Check Understanding Have small groups work together to build short *a* and short *i* words with magnetic letters or other materials. This time, they can write new words in the Word Bank section of their journals and add pictures.

Extend Practice Have children build words using *van, rip, cab,* and *lip.* Have children blend the words. Model blending as needed. Then ask children to read the sentence <u>Here</u> <u>is</u> <u>my</u> pig. Remind them to blend the sounds for *pig.* (Underlined words are from the Word Wall.)

INDEPENDENT WRITING
Journals

OBJECTIVES
- Write independently.

Materials
- journals

Preparing to Write
- Together, reread the class story you composed this week.
- Then recall your discussions about trains, race cars, and other vehicles.

Writing Independently
- Pass out the journals.
- Let's think about some of the things we learned this week. What kind of wheels could you write about? What did you learn about the beginning of a story? Maybe you'll decide to draw a vehicle that has a problem and then write about it.
- Encourage children to revisit *Vroom, Chugga, Vroom-Vroom* and *Cool Wheels!* for writing ideas.
- Remind children that they can use words from the Word Wall as well as the charts with words that tell where. Remind children to use what they know about letter sounds to help them spell other words.
- If time permits, allow children to share what they've written with the class.

Portfolio Opportunity

Mark journal entries you would like to share with parents. Occasionally allow children to mark their best efforts or favorite works for sharing as well.

▲ **ON LEVEL**

Going for a Ride

by Courtney Kim

Going for a Ride

Summary: *This nonfiction book describes a variety of ways to go for a ride. Children and adults ride on a bike, on a sled, in a car, in a truck, in a van, in a bus, and on a scooter.*

Story Words

We *p. 2*

can *p. 2*

ride *p. 2*

High-Frequency Words

New Words

have *p. 2*

for *p. 2*

Review Words

a *p. 2*

go *p. 2*

I *p. 8*

like *p. 8*

to *p. 8*

Building Background and Vocabulary

Tell children that this story is about children and adults who go for rides on all kinds of vehicles. Preview the photographs. Encourage children to share their own experiences riding or being taken for a ride on different kinds of vehicles. Ask them to list the kinds of vehicles they have driven themselves and the kinds of vehicles in which they have been passengers.

Comprehension Skill: Cause and Effect

Read together the Strategy Focus on the book flap. Remind children to use the strategy and to notice, as they read the story, what causes things to happen.

Responding

Discussing the Book Ask children to share their personal responses to the book. Begin by asking them to talk about what they liked best about the story or what they found the most interesting. Have children point to sentences or photographs they especially enjoyed. Ask children to talk about the rides in the story that they have experienced, and the rides they would like to try someday.

Responding Have children answer the questions on the inside back cover. Then help them complete the Writing and Drawing activity. Have children take turns explaining their drawings to the class, and reading the labels they have written. Ask children to help you categorize the drawings. For example, have children who wrote about bikes stand together in a group.

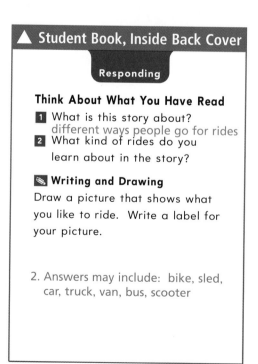

▲ **Student Book, Inside Back Cover**

Responding

Think About What You Have Read
1. What is this story about?
   different ways people go for rides
2. What kind of rides do you learn about in the story?

✎ **Writing and Drawing**
Draw a picture that shows what you like to ride. Write a label for your picture.

2. Answers may include: bike, sled, car, truck, van, bus, scooter

🎯 Building Fluency

Model Ask children to follow along as you reread pages 2 and 3 to them. Point out that the first three words, *We have a*, on the two pages are the same. Tell children that these words begin every page in the book until the last page. Then read the second sentence on page 2, *We can go for a ride*. Tell children that this whole sentence is the second sentence on every page in the book until the last page.

Practice Divide the group into two smaller groups and continue reading the book aloud until page 7. For each page, have one group read the first sentence, while the other group reads the second sentence.

Oral Language Development

Vehicle Words Discuss with children words that name vehicles. Explain that these words tell the different ways people can travel, or go for a ride. Have children page through the story, pointing to the word that tells a way to travel on each page (*bike, sled, car, truck, van, bus, scooter*). Have volunteers talk about their own experiences with the specific vehicle shown in each photograph.

Practice Have children practice using the vehicle words. Name different vehicles, and ask the class to tell something about each one, such as how many wheels it has, or whether it travels on the ground, in the air, or on water.

High-Frequency Words

New Words: *have, for*   Review Words: *a, go, I, like, to*

Display the Word Cards for *have* and *for*. Read the words aloud. Ask children to listen for the words as you read page 2 in *Going for a Ride*. Then have them turn to page 4 in the story. Point to the Word Cards and ask children to point to the words *have* and *for* in the text. Then ask children to read the two sentences on the page together.

Display the Word Card for *like*. Ask children to spell the word as you point to the letters. Then have children turn to page 8 in the book. Ask them to listen for the word *like* as you read *I like to go for a ride*. Ask children to take turns reading the sentence.

have	for	like

Lesson Overview

Literature

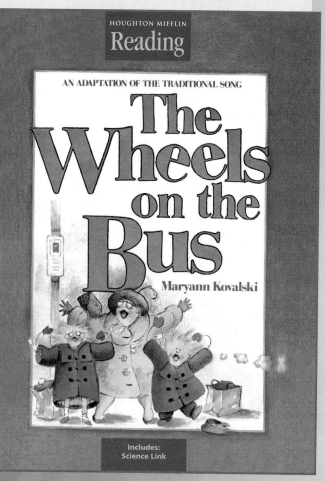

HOUGHTON MIFFLIN
Reading

AN ADAPTATION OF THE TRADITIONAL SONG

The Wheels on the Bus

Maryann Kovalski

Includes:
Science Link

HOUGHTON MIFFLIN
Reading

VROOM, CHUGGA, VROOM-VROOM

written by Anne Miranda
illustrated by David Murphy

Includes:
Science Link

1 Teacher Read Aloud
- *Mr. Gumpy's Motor Car*

2 Big Books
- *The Wheels on the Bus*

- *Vroom, Chugga, Vroom-Vroom*

3 Decodable Text
Phonics Library
- "Zig Pig and Dan Cat"

Zig Pig and Dan Cat
by Amy Griffin
illustrated by Amiko Hirao

4 Science Links

Look for Wheels

Cool Wheels!

These Links appear after the main
Big Book selections.

Leveled Books

Vocabulary Reader

- Below Level, ELL
- Lesson

Leveled Reader

- On Level, Above Level
- Lesson
- Take-Home Version

Plus!
Online Leveled Books

Instructional Support

Planning and Practice

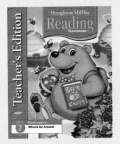

Tennessee Teacher's Edition

Teacher's Resources

Alphafriends

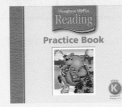

Practice book

Differentiated Instruction

Intervention/Extra Support

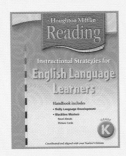

English Language Learners

Challenge

Ready-Made Centers

Phonics Center

Building Vocabulary

Reading in Science and Social Studies
- 30 books and activities
- support for Tennessee content standards

Hands-On Literacy Centers for Week 3
- activities
- manipulatives
- routines

Technology

 **Audio Selections**
The Wheels on the Bus

Vroom, Chugga, Vroom-Vroom

www.eduplace.com
- over 1,000 Online Leveled Books

Daily Lesson Plans

 **Technology**

Lesson Planner CD-ROM allows you to customize the chart below to develop your own lesson plans.

T Skill tested on Weekly or Theme Skills Test and/or Integrated Theme Test

 Tennessee Curriculum Standards indicated in blue.

WEEK 3   **DAILY LESSON PLANS**

60–90 minutes

Learning to Read

Phonemic Awareness

Phonics

High-Frequency Words

Comprehension

Concepts of Print

 Vocabulary Reader — We Ride!

The Toy Store

Leveled Reader

30–45 minutes

Word Work

High-Frequency Word Practice

Building Words

30–45 minutes

Writing and Oral Language

Vocabulary

Writing

Listening/Speaking/Viewing

DAY 1

K.1.01.e, K.1.07.d, K.1.07.e
Daily Routines, *T140–T141*
Calendar, Message, High-Frequency Words

Phonemic Awareness T K.1.04.b, K.1.04.c

Teacher Read Aloud, *T142–T145* K.1.02

Comprehension Strategy, *T142* K.1.09.a
Question

Comprehension Skill, *T142*
Making Predictions T K.1.08.c, K.1.09.a

Phonemic Awareness, *T146–T147*
Beginning Sounds /d/, /z/ **T** K.1.04.f

Leveled Reader
K.1.04, K.1.05, K.1.09

High-Frequency Word Practice, *T148*
Words: *a, for, have, I, my* K.1.07.e, K.3.03

Oral Language: Vocabulary, *T149*
Using Opposites K.1.01.f, K.1.07

Vocabulary Reader K.1.07

DAY 2

K.1.04.f, K.1.07.d, K.1.07.e
Daily Routines, *T150–T151*
Calendar, Message, High-Frequency Words

Phonemic Awareness T
K.1.04.b, K.1.04.c

Reading the Big Book, *T152–T153* K.1.06

Comprehension Strategy, *T152, T153*
Question K.1.09.a

Comprehension Skill, *T152, T153*
Making Predictions **T** K.1.08.c, K.1.09.a

Concepts of Print, *T153* K.1.05.b, K.1.05.c, K.1.07
Match Spoken Words to Print; Match Words **T**

Phonics, *T154–T155* K.1.05.b, K.1.05.c
Review Initial Consonants *d, z* **T**

High-Frequency Words, *T156–T157*
Review Words: *for, have* **T** K.1.07.e, K.3.03

Leveled Reader
K.1.04, K.1.05, K.1.09

High-Frequency Word Practice, *T158*
Building Sentences K.1.07.e, K.3.03, K.3.04.b

Vocabulary Reader K.1.07

Vocabulary Expansion, *T159* K.1.07
Words for Travel

Listening/Speaking/Viewing, *T159*
K.1.01.f, K.2.01.a

The Wheels on the Bus

 Half-Day Kindergarten

Focus on lessons for tested skills marked with **T**. Then choose other activities as time allows.

T134   **THEME 7: Wheels Go Around**

Target Skills of the Week

Phonemic Awareness	Blending Phonemes; Segmenting Phonemes
Phonics	Review Initial Consonants: *D, d, z*; Short *a* or *i* Words
Comprehension	Making Predictions; Question; Summarize
Vocabulary	High-Frequency Words; Opposites; Words for Travel
Fluency	Phonics Library; On My Way Practice Reader

DAY 3

K.1.04.f, K.1.07.d, K.1.07.e

Daily Routines,
T160–T161
Calendar, Message, High-Frequency Words

Phonemic Awareness T
K.1.04.b, K.1.04.c
Reading the Big Book, *T162–T163* K.1.06

Comprehension Strategy, *T162, T163*
Question K.1.09.a

Comprehension Skill, *T162, T163*
Making Predictions T K.1.08.c, K.1.09.a

Concepts of Print, *T163* K.1.05.b, K.1.05.c, K.1.07
Match Spoken Words to Print; Match Words T

Phonics, *T164* K.1.05.b, K.1.05.c
Review Consonants *d* and *z*; Blend Short *i* Words T

Reading Decodable Text, *T165–T167*
"Zig Pig and Dan Cat" K.1.05.b, K.1.05.c

Vocabulary Reader K.1.07

Leveled Reader
K.1.04, K.1.05, K.1.09

Building Words, *T168* K.1.05.b, K.1.05.c, K.1.05.d
Words with Short *i*

Shared Writing, *T169* K.2.01.d, K.2.02.c, K.2.08
Writing a Report

DAY 4

Daily Routines,
T170–T171
Calendar, Message, High-Frequency Words K.1.01.e, K.1.04.f, K.1.07

Phonemic Awareness T
K.1.04.b, K.1.04.c
Reading the Links, *T172–T173* K.1.09
Look for Wheels
Cool Wheels!

Comprehension Strategy, *T172* K.1.09.b
Summarize

Comprehension Skill, *T172–T173*
Making Predictions T K.1.08.c, K.1.09.a

Concepts of Print, *T172* K.1.05.b, K.1.05.c, K.1.07
Match Spoken Words to Print; Match Words T

Phonics, *T174–T175* K.1.05.b, K.1.05.c
Blending Short *i* Words T

Vocabulary Reader K.1.07

Leveled Reader
K.1.04, K.1.05, K.1.09

Building Words, *T176* K.1.05.b, K.1.05.c, K.1.05.d
Words with Short *i* or Short *a*

Interactive Writing, *T177* K.2.01.d, K.2.02.c, K.2.08
Writing a Report

DAY 5

Daily Routines,
T178–T179 K.1.01.e, K.1.03.f, K.1.07
Calendar, Message, High-Frequency Words

Phonemic Awareness T
K.1.04.c
Revisiting the Literature, *T180* K.1.01.e, K.1.09

Comprehension Skill, *T180*
Making Predictions T K.1.08.c, K.1.09.a

On My Way Practice Reader, *T181* K.1.08
Dig, Zig Pig!

Phonics Review, *T182* K.1.05.b, K.1.05.c
Familiar Consonants;
Short *i* or Short *a* Words T

High-Frequency Word Review, *T183* K.1.07.e, K.3.03
Words: *I, see, my, like, a, to, and, go, is, here, for, have* T

Vocabulary Reader K.1.07

Leveled Reader
K.1.04, K.1.05, K.1.09

Building Words, *T184* K.1.05.b, K.1.05.c, K.1.05.d
Words with Short *i* or Short *a*

Independent Writing, *T185* K.2.09.b, K.2.11.a
Journals: Favorite Kinds of Wheels

Concepts of Print lessons teach important foundational skills for Phonics.

Managing Flexible Groups

Leveled Instruction and Leveled Practice

WHOLE CLASS

DAY 1

- Daily Routines (TE pp. T140–T141)
- Teacher Read Aloud: *Mr. Gumpy's Motor Car* (TE pp. T142–T145)
- Phonemic Awareness (TE pp. T146–T147)

DAY 2

- Daily Routines (TE pp. T150–T151)
- Big Book: *The Wheels on the Bus* (TE pp. T152–T153)
- Phonics Lesson (TE pp. T154–T155)
- High-Frequency Word Lesson (TE pp. T156–T157)

SMALL GROUPS

Organize small groups according to children's needs.

DAY 1

TEACHER-LED GROUPS

- Begin Practice Book pp. 51, 52, 53, 54. (TE pp. T143, T147)
- Introduce Phonics Center. (TE p. T147)
- Leveled Reader

DAY 2

TEACHER-LED GROUPS

- Begin Practice Book pp. 55, 56. (TE pp. T155, T157)
- Review letters *D, d, Z, z*; begin handwriting Blackline Masters 160, 172 or 186, 208. (TE p. T155)
- Introduce Phonics Center. (TE p. T155)
- Leveled Reader
- Vocabulary Reader

INDEPENDENT GROUPS

- Complete Practice Book pp. 51, 52, 53, 54. (TE pp. T143, T147)
- Use Phonics Center. (TE p. T147)

INDEPENDENT GROUPS

- Complete Practice Book pp. 55, 56. (TE pp. T155, T157)
- Complete Blackline Masters 160, 172 or 186, 208.
- Use Phonics Center. (TE p. T155)

English Language Learners
Support is provided in the Reaching All Learners notes throughout the week.

- Complete Practice Book pages 51–60.
- Reread familiar Phonics Library stories.
- Share trade books from Leveled Bibliography. (See pp. T4–T5)
- Use the Phonics Center and other Centers. (See pp. T138–T139)

DAY 3

- Daily Routines (TE pp. T160–T161)
- Big Book: *Vroom, Chugga, Vroom-Vroom* (TE pp. T162–T163)
- Phonics Lesson (TE p. T164)

TEACHER-LED GROUPS

- Begin Practice Book pp. 57, 58. (TE pp. T163, T164)
- Write letters *I, i*; begin handwriting Blackline Master 165 or 191.
- Read Phonics Library: "Zig Pig and Dan Cat." (TE pp. T165–T167)
- Leveled Reader
- Vocabulary Reader

INDEPENDENT GROUPS

- Complete Practice Book pp. 57, 58. (TE pp. T163, T164)
- Complete Blackline Master 165 or 191.
- **Fluency Practice** Reread Phonics Library: "Zig Pig and Dan Cat." (TE pp. T165–T167)

DAY 4

- Daily Routines (TE pp. T170–T171)
- Science Links
  Look for Wheels (TE p. T172)
  Cool Wheels! (TE p. T173)
- Phonics Lesson (TE pp. T174–T175)

TEACHER-LED GROUPS

- Begin Practice Book p. 59. (TE p. T175)
- Introduce the Phonics Center. (TE p. T175)
- Leveled Reader
- Vocabulary Reader

INDEPENDENT GROUPS

- Complete Practice Book p. 59. (TE p. T175)
- **Fluency Practice** Color and reread Phonics Library: "Zig Pig and Dan Cat." (TE pp. T165–T167)
- Use Phonics Center. (TE p. T175)

DAY 5

- Daily Routines (TE pp. T178–T179)
- Rereading (TE p. T180)
- On My Way Practice Reader (TE p. T181)
- Phonics and High-Frequency Word Review (TE pp. T182–T183)

TEACHER-LED GROUPS

- Begin Practice Book p. 60. (TE p. T183)
- **Fluency Practice** Reread the Take-Home version of "Zig Pig and Dan Cat."
- Leveled Reader
- Vocabulary Reader

INDEPENDENT GROUPS

- Complete Practice Book p. 60. (TE p. T183)
- **Fluency Practice** Reread a favorite Phonics Library or Leveled Reader story.

- Complete penmanship practice (Teacher's Resource Blackline Masters 160, 172 or 186, 208 and 165 or 191).
- Retell or reread Little Big Books.
- Listen to Big Book Audio CD's.

Turn the page for more independent activities.

Managing Flexible Groups T137

Ready-Made for Tennessee

Independent Activities

Building Vocabulary

Center Activity 21

ELA.K.1.01.a, ELA.K.1.01.e,
ELA.K.1.01.f, ELA.K.1.01.g,
ELA.K.1.07.a, ELA.K.1.07.b

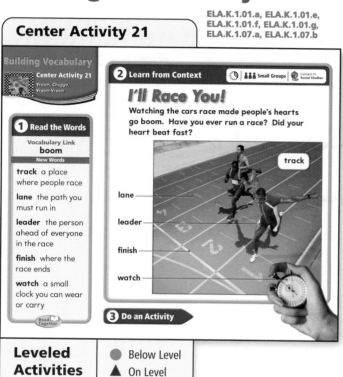

Building Vocabulary
Center Activity 21
Vroom, Chugga,
Vroom-Vroom

1 Read the Words

Vocabulary Link
boom
New Words

track a place where people race

lane the path you must run in

leader the person ahead of everyone in the race

finish where the race ends

watch a small clock you can wear or carry

Read Together

2 Learn from Context   🕐 | 👥👥👥 Small Groups | 🌐 Connect to Social Studies

I'll Race You!

Watching the cars race made people's hearts go boom. Have you ever run a race? Did your heart beat fast?

track

lane
leader
finish
watch

3 Do an Activity

Leveled Activities
on back of card

● Below Level
▲ On Level
■ Above Level

Hands-On Literacy Centers

Challenge and Routine Cards

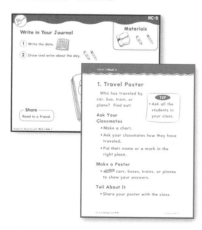

Write in Your Journal
① Write the date.
② Draw and write about the day.

Share
Read to a friend.

1. Travel Poster
Who has traveled by car, bus, train, or plane? Find out!

TIP
• Ask all the students in your class.

Ask Your Classmates
• Make a chart.
• Ask your classmates how they have traveled.
• Put their name or a mark in the right place.

Make a Poster
• cars, buses, trains, or planes to show your answers.

Tell About It
• Share your poster with the class.

Manipulatives

for

Reading in Social Studies

Independent Book
Fun and Games: Then and Now
Students apply comprehension skills to nonfiction text.

Fun and Games
Then and Now

By Dana Zachary

SS.K.5.02.a, ELA.K.1.11.b

Center Activity 21

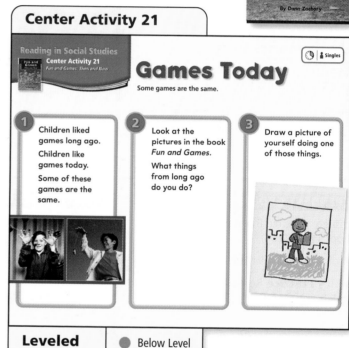

Reading in Social Studies
Center Activity 21
Fun and Games: Then and Now

🕐 | 👤 Singles

Games Today

Some games are the same.

1 Children liked games long ago.
Children like games today.
Some of these games are the same.

2 Look at the pictures in the book *Fun and Games.*
What things from long ago do you do?

3 Draw a picture of yourself doing one of those things.

Leveled Activities
on back of card

● Below Level
▲ On Level
■ Above Level

More Nonfiction Reading

30 topics aligned with **Tennessee** Science and Social Studies standards!

Setting Up Centers

Phonics Center

Materials
Phonics Center materials for
Theme 7, Week 3

This week children sort **Picture Cards** by initial sound and letter. They make words with the letters *b*, *d*, *p* and short *i*. They also build sentences with **Word** and **Picture Cards**. Prepare materials for Days 1, 2, and 4. See pages T147, T155, and T175 for this week's **Phonics Center** activities.

Art Center

Materials
drawing paper, crayons and markers

Children draw and label pictures of wheels at work, their favorite vehicle, and their own favorite "cool wheels." See pages T153, T159, T163, and T173 for this week's Art Center activities.

SS.K.1.02

Writing Center

Materials
lined and unlined writing paper, drawing paper, crayons or markers

---

Children illustrate and label a pair of opposites. They draw and write about jobs they would enjoy. Later they draw pictures with captions to go with a class report. See pages T149 and T177 for this week's Writing Center activities.

SS.K.2.01a, SS.K.2.01b, SS.K.2.03a, SS.K.2.03c

DAY 1
week 3

Day at a Glance
T140–T149

Learning to Read

Teacher Read Aloud, *T142*
Phonemic Awareness: */d/, /z/,* *T146*

Word Work

High-Frequency Word Practice, *T148*

Writing & Oral Language

Oral Language, *T149*

Daily Routines

Calendar

Sunday	Monday	Tuesday	Wednesday	Thursday	Friday	Saturday
			1	2	3	4
5	6	7	8	9	10	11
12	13	14	15	16	17	18
19	20	21	22	23	24	25
26	27	28	29	30	31	

Reading the Calendar After children describe the day's weather, talk about opposites, or things that are completely different. Suggest an opposite for today's weather. For example, if today is rainy, say that the opposite weather would be sunny. Continue with: *day/night, hot/cold, wet/dry, mild/wild, dark/light, cloudy/clear.*

hot/cold   *cloudy/clear*
wet/dry   *rainy/sunny*   *day/night*

Daily Message

Modeled Writing
Tie today's message to the theme by asking if any children traveled on wheels over the weekend. As children tell about the vehicles, incorporate the responses into the day's message.

Kendra and Jamal rode on a bus. Sandy, Marco, and Alyssa rode on a subway train.

Word Wall

High-Frequency Words Choose an individual to point to and read the two words that were added to the Word Wall in this theme. (for, have) Continue reading the other word groups.

for   have

Word Cards for these words appear on pages R8–R10.

Daily Phonemic Awareness

Blending and Segmenting Phonemes

- Read "Notice" on page 20 of *Higglety Pigglety*. Play a "break-apart" game. I will break apart a word from the poem. Listen to the sounds. See if you can put them back together to make a word: /d/ /ŏ/ /g/. Say the sounds with me: /d/ /ŏ/ /g/. What is the word? (dog) Continue, segmenting the words *cat, hat,* and *got*.

- Now reverse the procedure. Say some other two- or three-sound words, and have partners count and say the separate sounds.

Notice

I have a dog,
I had a cat.
I've got a frog
Inside my hat.

by David McCord

20

Higglety Pigglety: A Book of Rhymes, page 20

Getting Ready to Learn

To help children plan their day, tell them that they will—

- listen to a story called *Mr. Gumpy's Motor Car.*

- revisit two Alphafriends.

- act out a story in the Dramatic Play Center.

OBJECTIVES

- Develop oral language (listening, responding).
- Preview comprehension skill.

Read Aloud

Mr. Grumpy's Motor Car

Selection Summary The sun is shining when Mr. Gumpy agrees to take his children and the animals for a car ride. But when the skies open up and the road turns muddy, it takes the help of all the passengers to free the car from the mud.

Key Concept Many hands make easy work.

Teacher Read Aloud

Building Background

Explain that today's story is about a car. Invite children to tell about car rides they have shared with family or friends. Were you taking a drive for fun or did you have a place to go to? How many people went for the ride? What was the weather like?

 COMPREHENSION SKILL

Making Predictions

Teacher Modeling Display the picture on T145 and read the title, *Mr. Gumpy's Motor Car.* Then model how to make predictions about the story.

Think Aloud The title tells me the story is about Mr. Gumpy's motor car. In the picture, I see a man and a car. The man must be Mr. Gumpy, and the motor car must be his. I also see that Mr. Gumpy is holding a case, so maybe he is going somewhere. I will read the story to find out if my prediction is right.

 COMPREHENSION STRATEGY

Question

Teacher Modeling Model how to pose questions you'd like the story to answer.

Think Aloud Asking questions before you read can help you understand a story better and make it even more interesting. I wonder: Where does Mr. Gumpy go on his car ride? Who does he take with him? Let's listen for the answers as I read.

Listening to the Story

Fold your Teacher's Edition so that children can see page T145 as you read. Note that the art is also available on the back of the Theme Poster.

Read the story with expression. As you read the long list of characters, count them off on your fingers and invite children to do the same. Pause for the discussion points, asking children to tell what might happen next. Read on to check their predictions.

Responding

Oral Language: Summarizing the Story Use these prompts to help children summarize.

- What did Mr. Gumpy decide to do at the beginning of the story? Who wanted to come along?

- What prediction did Mr. Gumpy make when he saw the clouds? Was he right? What happened next?

- What reasons did the children and the animals give for not wanting to push the motor car? How did the car finally get out of the mud?

- What do you think will happen the next time Mr. Gumpy needs help? Why?

Children who enjoyed this story may also enjoy another John Burningham book, *Mr. Gumpy's Outing*, a story about a boat ride that ends with a real splash.

Practice Book Children will complete **Practice Book** pages 51–52 during small group time.

Dramatic Play Center

Materials Blackline Masters 108–109

Give each child a character's picture from **Blackline Masters 108–109**. Then use yarn to outline an area in the Center to be Mr. Gumpy's motor car. Children can hold the characters and crowd into the car for an afternoon drive across the fields. Reread the story, having children supply appropriate sound effects.

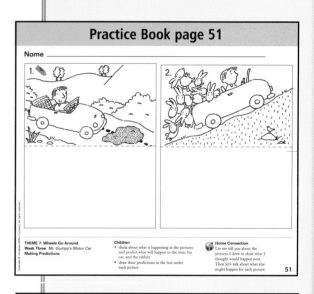

Practice Book page 51

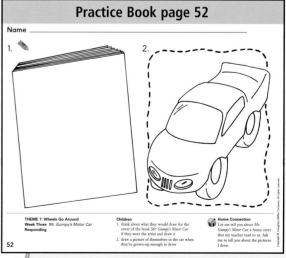

Practice Book page 52

Mr. Gumpy's Motor Car

By John Burningham

A Contemporary British Tale

Mr. Gumpy was going for a ride in his car. He drove out of the gate and down the lane.

"May we come too?" said the children.

"May we?" said the rabbit, the cat, the dog, the pig, the sheep, the chickens, the calf, and the goat.

"All right," said Mr. Gumpy. "But it will be a squash."

And they all piled in.

"It's a lovely day," said Mr. Gumpy. "Let's take the old dirt road across the fields."

For a while they drove along happily. The sun shone, the engine chugged, and everyone was enjoying the ride.

"I don't like the look of those clouds. I think it's going to rain," said Mr. Gumpy.

Very soon the dark clouds were right overhead. Mr. Gumpy stopped the car. He jumped out, put up the top, and down came the rain.

The road grew muddier and muddier, and the wheels began to spin. Mr. Gumpy looked at the hill ahead. **(Say: That sounds like trouble! What do you think Mr. Gumpy will do? Let's read on and find the answer.)**

"Some of you will have to get out and push," he said.

"Not me," said the goat. "I am too old."

"Not me," said the calf. "I am too young."

"Not us," said the chickens. "We can't push."

"Not me," said the sheep. "I might catch a cold."

"Not me," said the pig. "I've a bone in my trotter."

"Not me," said the dog. "But I'll drive if you like."

"Not me," said the cat. "It would ruin my fur."

"Not me," said the rabbit. "I'm not very well."

"Not me," said the girl. "He's stronger."

"Not me," said the boy. "She's bigger." **(Say: Oh, no! No one wanted to help! What will happen to the car?)**

The wheels churned . . .

The car sank deeper into the mud.

"Now we're really stuck," said Mr. Gumpy.

(Ask: Were we right? Now I wonder how they will get out of this mess! Let's read on to find out.)

They all got out and pushed.

They pushed and shoved and heaved and strained and gasped and slipped and slithered and squelched. Slowly the car began to move . . .

"Don't stop!" cried Mr. Gumpy. "Keep it up! We're nearly there."

Everyone gave a mighty heave—the tires gripped . . .

The car edged its way to the top of the hill. They looked up and saw that the sun was shining again. It began to get hot.

"We'll drive home across the bridge," said Mr. Gumpy. "Then you can go for a swim." And they did.

After a while it was time to go home.

"Good-bye," said Mr. Gumpy. "Come for a drive another day."

OBJECTIVES

- Identify pictures whose names begin with /d/, /z/.

Materials

- **Alphafriend Cards** *Dudley Duck, Reggie Rooster, Zelda Zebra*
- **Alphafriend CD** Theme 7
- **Alphafolder** *Dudley Duck, Zelda Zebra*
- **Picture Cards** for *d, r, z*
- **Phonics Center** Theme 7, Week 3, Day 1

Alphafolder *Dudley Duck*

Alphafolder *Zelda Zebra*

Home Connection

Hand out the take-home versions of Dudley Duck's Song and Zelda Zebra's Song. Ask children to share the songs with their families. (See **Alphafriends Blackline Masters.**)

PHONEMIC AWARENESS
Beginning Sound

❶ Teach

Revisit Alphafriends: Dudley Duck and Zelda Zebra.

Adapt the Alphafriend routine to review Dudley Duck and Zelda Zebra.

▶ **Alphafriend Riddles** Read these clues:

- This Alphafriend's sound is /d/. He quacks and swims. **Call on children until they name** *duck.*

- This Alphafriend's sound is /z/. She has black and white stripes. **Call on children until they name** *zebra.*

▶ **Pocket Chart** Display Dudley Duck in the pocket chart. Say his name, emphasizing the /d/ sound and having children echo. Then display Zelda Zebra, stretching the /z/ sound as you say her name. Remind children that Dudley's sound is /d/ and Zelda's sound is /z/.

▶ **Alphafriend CD** Play Dudley Duck's song. Invite children to sing along and make "duck bills" when they hear words that start with /d/.

▶ **Alphafolder** Have children review the illustration and name the /d/ pictures.

▶ **Summarize**

- What is our Alphafriend's name? What is his sound?

- What words in his song start with /d/?

- What should we remember when we look at Dudley Duck? (the /d/ sound)

Repeat the process to review Zelda Zebra's sound.

❷ Guided Practice

Listen for /d/ and /z/ and compare and review /r/. Add Alphafriend *Reggie Rooster* opposite *Dudley Duck* and *Zelda Zebra*. Review each character's sound.

Hold up Picture Cards one at a time. Children signal "thumbs up" for picture names that start like Dudley's name and a child puts those cards below Dudley's picture. For "thumbs down" words, children put cards below the correct Alphafriend.

Pictures: *desk, zigzag, rock, doll, rope, zipper, rug, doll, zip*

Tell children that they will sort more pictures in the **Phonics Center** today.

❸ Apply

Have children complete **Practice Book** pages 53–54 at small group time.

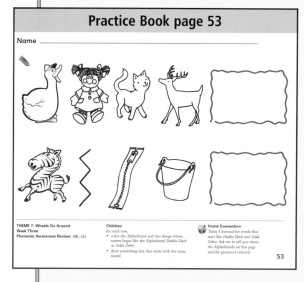

Practice Book page 53

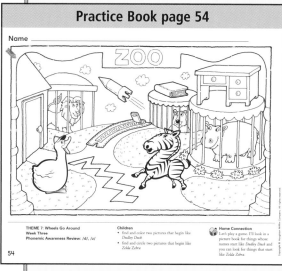

Practice Book page 54

ABC Phonics Center

Materials Phonics Center materials for Theme 7, Week 3, Day 1

Display Day 1 Direction Chart. Children put *Dudley Duck, Zelda Zebra* and *Reggie Rooster* (without letters) in separate sections of Workmat 3. Then they sort remaining pictures by initial sound: /d/, /z/, and /r/.

OBJECTIVES

- Read high-frequency words.
- Create and write sentences with high-frequency words.

Materials

- *Higglety Pigglety: A Book of Rhymes,* page 16
- **Word Cards** *a, for, have, I, my*
- **Picture Cards** *bed, doll, jam, toast*
- **Punctuation Card** period

High-Frequency Words

Display and read the Word Cards for *have* and *for* in a pocket chart.

- Call on children to identify each word and to match it on the Word Wall.

Higglety Pigglety: A Book of Rhymes, page 16

- Remind children that these are words they often see in books. I'll read a poem. You listen to hear if these words are in it.

- Read "Baa, Baa, Black Sheep" on page 16 of *Higglety Pigglety.* Did you hear the words *have* and *for?* Read the poem line for line and have children match the **Word Cards** to those words in the poem.

Have children write sentences.

- Display the **Word Cards** and **Picture Cards** from the Materials list. Begin a sentence with *I have,* and then ask children to choose cards to complete the sentence in different ways.

- Distribute paper and have children write and illustrate one of the sentences or create their own.

ORAL LANGUAGE: VOCABULARY
Using Opposites

OBJECTIVES

• Name and illustrate opposites.

❶ Teach

Review *Mr. Gumpy's Motor Car*.

• Remind children that the characters in *Mr. Gumpy's Motor Car* had different reasons for not wanting to push the car.

• The goat said it was too old. The calf said it was too young. What do you know about the words *old* and *young*?

• If necessary, explain that the words are opposites, or words that mean completely different things. Offer more examples: *wet/dry, cold/hot, out/in, on/off.*

❷ Practice/Apply

Have children practice using opposites.

• Help children begin a list of opposites by rereading lines from the story that contain examples. List children's suggestions on a chart.

• Use prompts to help children brainstorm more opposites. Examples: What happens when a race car crosses the finish line first? (It wins.) What happens when it crosses last? (It loses.)

Opposites

old	young
rainy	sunny
stuck	loose
win	lose
fast	slow
full	empty
strong	weak
big	little

Writing Center

Put the chart in the Writing Center. Ask children to illustrate a pair of opposites and label their pictures.

big and little

DAY 2
week 3

Day at a Glance
T150–T159

Learning to Read

Big Book, *T152*

Phonics: Initial Consonants *d, z,* *T154*

High Frequency Words: *for, have,* *T156*

Word Work

High-Frequency Word Practice, *T158*

Writing & Oral Language

Vocabulary Expansion, *T159*

Daily Routines

Calendar

Reading the Calendar Play an opposites game after your calendar routine. Have a child say a word that describes today's weather and call on a classmate to say the word's opposite. Have other children point to and name sections of the calendar such as *top, left* side, *first* day of the week, *first* date in the month; classmates can name the opposites.

Daily Message

Interactive Writing As you write the daily message, have children help you. Ask them to supply initial and final consonants and to help you build and write short *i* words.

It is sunny today, with big white clouds.

Word Wall

High-Frequency Words Distribute cards for the Word Wall words. Have children match their cards to the same words on the Word Wall. After a match is made, have other children chant the spelling of the word: *a-n-d* spells *and; g-o* spells *go.*

go   and

Word Cards for these words appear on pages R8–R10.

Daily Phonemic Awareness

Blending and Segmenting Phonemes

- Read "To Market, To Market" on page 31 of *Higglety Pigglety.*

- Play a guessing game. Tell children that you will give them a clue about a word from the poem. When they know the answer, they should raise their hands.

- I'm thinking of a word. The sounds are /ĭ/ /z/. (is) When most hands are up, have children say the word together.

- Continue with other words from the poem: *to, hog, fat,* and *home.*

- Now reverse roles. Children can choose a word, tell you the number of sounds and name them, and ask you to guess the word.

TO MARKET, TO MARKET

To market, to market, to buy a fat pig,
Home again, home again, jiggety jig.
To market, to market, to buy a fat hog,
Home again, home again, jiggety jog.
To market, to market, to buy
a plum bun,
Home again, home again,
market is done.

a Mother Goose Rhyme

31

Higglety Pigglety: A Book of Rhymes, **page 31**

Getting Ready to Learn

To help children plan their day, tell them that they will–

- listen to a **Big Book:** *The Wheels on the Bus.*

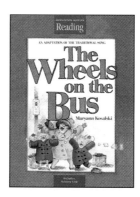

- review the letters *D, d* and *Z, z,* and sort words that begin with *d* and *z.*

- write about wheels in the Writing Center.

A ⊙ can help my dad.

OBJECTIVES

- Introduce concepts of print.
- Develop story language.
- Reinforce comprehension strategy and comprehension skill.

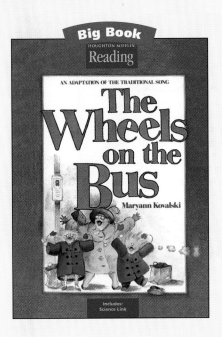

Big Book

HOUGHTON MIFFLIN
Reading

AN ADAPTATION OF THE TRADITIONAL SONG

The Wheels on the Bus

Maryann Kovalski

Includes:
Science Link

Extra Support/ Intervention

On a rereading of the story, children can sing the text using the pictures as prompts.

INSTRUCTION

Reading the Big Book

Building Background

Display *The Wheels on the Bus*. Call on children to share what they remember about the story. As we read the story this time, see if you can remember the things that happen on the old-fashioned bus.

 COMPREHENSION STRATEGY

Question

Teacher-Student Modeling Asking yourself questions and then looking for the answers in the story is a good way to understand it better. I want to know why the characters don't see or hear the bus when it comes. I'll look for the answer when we read. Ask children what questions they might ask about the characters or old-fashioned buses. Jot down their questions on chart paper and save them to answer after reading.

 COMPREHENSION SKILL

Making Predictions

Teacher-Student Modeling Remind children that while reading, they can use picture clues and what they have read so far to tell what might happen next. Display the book cover and read the title. What can you tell about this book from just the cover picture and the title?

Big Book Read Aloud

Reread the story, pausing for these discussion points:

 Concepts of Print

pages 12–13

Match spoken words to print; Match words

- There's a word on the page for every word I say. Say them with me as I point.
- Frame the word *and*. Ask children to say *and*, then find *and* three times. What other words on these pages match? Show me and I'll read them.

COMPREHENSION STRATEGY

Question

pages 24–25

● I see the real bus is here now. Look for the answer to my question: Why don't the characters see or hear that bus?

Responding

Oral Language: Personal Response Display the questions children posed before reading. Read each one and have children find the story page that shows the answer. Read the page and have children echo you.

Art Center

Materials drawing paper • crayons or markers

Have children draw pictures of wheels that help people in their neighborhoods or towns. Children can complete this sentence stem to caption their drawings: *A _____ can help _____.*

A 🚜 can help my dad.

Challenge

Small groups can work together to make books of wheels in their community. After drawing and captioning their pictures, have children decide whether any vehicles are missing. Then assemble the pages into a class book.

OBJECTIVES

- Identify words that begin with /d/, /z/
- Identify pictures whose names begin with *d* or *z*.
- Form the letters *D, d, Z, z*.

Materials

- **Alphafolders** *Dudley Duck, Zelda Zebra*
- **Alphafriend Card** *Dudley Duck, Zelda Zebra*
- **Letter Cards** *d, r, z*
- **Picture Cards** for *d, r, z*
- **Blackline Masters** 160, 182
- **Phonics Center** Theme 7, Week 3, Day 2

Extra Support/ Intervention

To help children remember the sounds for *d* and *z*, point out that the letters' names give clues to their sounds: *d*, /d/; *z*, /z/.

PHONICS
TARGET SKILL

Review Initial Consonants *d, z*

❶ Phonemic Awareness Warm-Up

Beginning Sound Read or sing the lyrics to Dudley Duck's song and have children echo it line-for-line. Have them listen for the /d/ words and pantomime a duck's bill for each one. Repeat for /z/ with Zelda Zebra's song, having children trace a zigzag motion in the air for each /z/. See Theme Resources page R2–R3 for music and lyrics.

❷ Teach Phonics

Beginning Letters Display the **Alphafriend Cards** *Dudley Duck* and *Zelda Zebra* and have children name the letters. What letter stands for the sound /d/, as in *duck*? What letter stands for the sound /z/, as in *zebra*? Which animal will help you remember the sound for *d*? the sound for *z*?

Tell children you want to write *duck* on the board. What letter should I write first? How did you know? Repeat with the word *zebra*.

❸ Guided Practice

Compare and Review: *d, z, r* In a pocket chart, display the **Letter Cards** as shown and the **Picture Cards** in random order. Review the sounds for *d, z,* and *r*. In turn, children can name a picture, say its beginning sound, and put the card below the right letter. Tell children they will sort more pictures in the **Phonics Center** today.

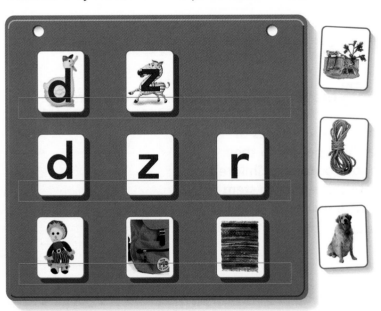

Penmanship Rhyme: D	Penmanship Rhyme: d	Penmanship Rhyme: Z	Penmanship Rhyme: z
Big *D* starts with a long line down. Go back to the top and curve all the way around: It's a *D*, a big *D*!	Start in the middle. Make a circle nice and round. Go up to the top and come straight down: It's a *d*, a small *d*, a small *d*!	From the top, zip right with a line. Slant down to the left, and zip right one more time: It's a *Z*, big *Z*, big *Z*!	From the middle, zip right with a line. Slant down to the left, and zip right one more time: It's a *z*, a small *z*, small *z*!

Penmanship: Writing *D, d; Z, z* Remind children that they have learned how to write the letters that stand for /d/: capital *D* and small *d*. They have also learned how to write the letters for /z/: capital *Z* and small *z*. Ask children to write each letter in the air as you recite the penmanship rhymes together.

④ Apply

Have children complete **Practice Book** page 55 at small group time. For additional penmanship practice assign **Blackline Master** 160. Penmanship practice for the continuous stroke style is available on **Blackline Master** 182.

Practice Book page 55

Name

THEME 7: Wheels Go Around
Week Three
Phonics Review: Initial Consonants *d, z*

Children
- use a yellow crayon to draw around *Dudley Duck* and to color all the pictures whose names begin with the sound for *d*
- use a blue crayon to draw around *Zelda Zebra* and to color all the pictures whose names begin with the sound for *z*
- write *d* beside yellow pictures and *z* beside blue pictures

Home Connection
Today I colored pictures of things whose names begin with the sounds for *z* and *d*. Let me tell you about the blue and yellow pictures.

55

Phonics Center

Materials	Phonics Center materials for Theme 7, Week 3, Day 2

Display Day 2 Direction Chart. Children put *Dudley Duck*, *Zelda Zebra*, and *Reggie Rooster* (with letters) in separate sections of Workmat 3. Then they sort remaining pictures by initial letter: *d*, *z*, and *r*.

OBJECTIVES

- Read and write the high-frequency words *for, have.*

Materials

- **Word Cards** *a, for, have, I, my*
- **Picture Cards** *bike, box, lock, toys*
- **Punctuation Card** period
- *Higglety Pigglety: A Book of Rhymes,* page 16

INSTRUCTION

HIGH-FREQUENCY WORDS
Review Words: *for, have*

❶ Teach

Review the words *for, have.* Tell children that today they will practice reading and writing two words that they will see often in stories. Say *for* and call on children to use the word in context.

- Write *for* on the board, and have children spell it as you point to the letters. Spell *for* with me, *f-o-r, for.*

- Lead children in a chant, clapping on each beat, to help them remember the spelling: *f-o-r, for; f-o-r, for.*

- Repeat for the word *have.*

Word Wall Have children find the words *for* and *have* on the Word Wall. Remind them to look there when they need to remember how to write the words.

❷ Guided Practice

Build these sentences one at a time. Ask children to take turns reading the sentences.

Place the pocket chart in the Writing Center along with additional **Picture Cards** so that children can practice building and reading sentences.

**Display *Higglety Pigglety:
A Book of Rhymes*, page 16.**

- Share the rhyme "Baa, Baa,
  Black Sheep."

- Reread the first two lines,
  tracking the print. Have children find and point to the
  word *have*.

- Repeat for the remaining
  lines in the rhyme, having
  children find the word *for*
  three times.

Higglety Pigglety: A Book of Rhymes,
page 16

❸ Apply

- Have children complete **Practice Book** page 56 at small group
  time.

- On Day 3 they will practice reading *for* and *have* in the Phonics
  Library story "Zig Pig and Dan Cat."

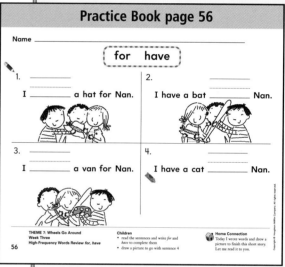

Practice Book page 56

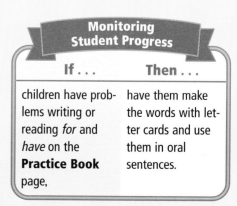

**Monitoring
Student Progress**

If . . .	Then . . .
children have prob-lems writing or reading *for* and *have* on the **Practice Book** page,	have them make the words with let-ter cards and use them in oral sentences.

PRACTICE

High-Frequency Words

Build sentences about colors used for drawing.

- Display the **Word Cards** and **Picture Cards** in random order. Put the **Word Card** *I* in the pocket chart, and read it.

- *I want the next word to be* have. *Who can find that word? That's right! This word is* have. *Now who can read my sentence so far?*

- Tell children you need a color word next. Have them choose a color word and add the words *for* and *a*.

- Children complete the sentence by choosing an appropriate **Picture Card**: *I have (yellow) for a _____.*

- Read the sentence together and then continue with new ones: *I have green for a leaf; I have black and white for a zebra.*

Have children write sentences.

- Have children copy a sentence from the pocket chart and illustrate it.

- Invite children to think of another color and write a sentence about what they could use it for in a drawing.

VOCABULARY EXPANSION
Words for Travel

TARGET SKILL

Listening/Speaking/Viewing

Review *The Wheels on the Bus*.

- Ask: How did Grandma, Jenny, and Joanna plan to get home? (by bus) How did they end up traveling at the end of the story? (by taxi)

- Write the words *bus* and *taxi* on chart paper and read them.

Discuss ways to travel.

- Have children name other ways people can travel. Add their suggestions to the chart paper list.

- Extend the discussion by asking: How can people travel across the water? How can they travel in the air?

Ways to Travel

bus	taxi	car
subway	train	trolley
bike	motorcycle	scooter
boat	airplane	helicopter

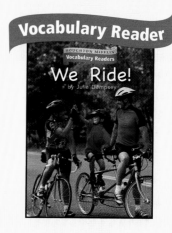

Art Center

On a few sheets of paper, write the stem *I can go for a ride in a ___*. Put the pages in the Art Center. Children can complete the sentence with a drawing of their favorite vehicle.

I can go for a ride in a van.

OBJECTIVES
- Brainstorm ways to travel.

Vocabulary Support

The Vocabulary Reader can be used to develop and reinforce vocabulary related to the instruction for this week.

Vocabulary Reader

HOUGHTON MIFFLIN
Vocabulary Readers
We Ride!
by Julie Dempsey

REACHING ALL LEARNERS

English Language Learners

As you discuss the ways people travel, English language learners can refer to the chart for help in communicating their ideas. Ask questions such as: *Have you been in a taxi? Who has been on a subway? Which is more fun, a boat or an airplane?* Emphasize the difference between prepositions such as *in* and *on*.

Vocabulary T159

Day at a Glance
T160–T169

Learning to Read

Big Book, *T162*

Phonics: Reviewing Consonant *d* **and** *z;* **Blending Short** *i* **Words,** *T164*

Word Work

Building Words, *T168*

Writing & Oral Language

Shared Writing, *T169*

Daily Routines

Calendar

Reading the Calendar Call on children to report on the "weather race." How many sunny days have we had so far? How many rainy days? How many more sunny days do we need before sunny days pass rainy days?

Sunday	Monday	Tuesday	Wednesday	Thursday	Friday	Saturday
			1	2	3	4
5	6	7	8	9	10	11
12	13	14	15	16	17	18
19	20	21	22	23	24	25
26	27	28	29	30	31	

Weather Race

Sunny	Rainy	Snowy
卌 I	卌	卌

Daily Message

Interactive Writing Refer to the calendar activity in the daily message. Provide opportunities for children to share in the writing of initial consonants, high-frequency words, words from known families, and end punctuation.

We are having a weather race. Which kind will win? Let's read about a race today.

Word Wall

High-Frequency Words Have children take turns finding Word Wall words with a pointer as you call them out.

to	and	here

Word Cards for these words appear on pages R8–R10.

Daily Phonemic Awareness

Blending and Segmenting Phonemes

Read "Hey, Diddle, Diddle" on page 32 of *Higglety Pigglety*.

- What is this word from the poem? Put these sounds together: /c/ /ă/ /t/. What word is that? (cat) Continue with *cow, dog,* and *ran*.

- Next, say these whole words and have children count and say the separate sounds: *moon, see, cat,* and *hey*.

Higglety Pigglety: A Book of Rhymes,
page 32

Getting Ready to Learn

To help children plan their day, tell them that they will—

- listen to the **Big Book:** *Vroom, Chugga, Vroom-Vroom.*

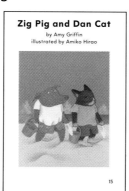

- read a story called "Zig Pig and Dan Cat."

- explore jobs in the Art Center.

OBJECTIVES

- Introduce concepts of print.
- Develop story language.
- Reinforce comprehension strategy and comprehension skill.

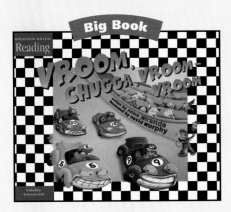

INSTRUCTION

Reading the Big Book

Building Background

Display *Vroom, Chugga, Vroom-Vroom.* Have children share what they remember about the race.

Place a flannel board near the book, and distribute numeral cards for 1–20. Tell children that as their car numbers are named in the beginning of the story, they should put the numbers in a column on the flannel board.

 COMPREHENSION STRATEGY

Question

Student Modeling Page through the first few pages of *Vroom, Chugga, Vroom-Vroom.* Ask children what questions they have about a car race that the text and the pictures might answer.

 COMPREHENSION SKILL

Making Predictions

Student Modeling What predictions could you make about *Vroom, Chugga, Vroom-Vroom* from the title and the picture on the cover? Why? (Sample clues about a car race: cars' positions, numbers on the cars, fans, the starter, a checked border that looks like the finish-line flag.)

Big Book Read Aloud

Reread the story, pausing for children to put numerals on the flannel board and to discuss these points:

CRITICAL THINKING

Guiding Comprehension

pages 14–17

NOTING DETAILS Remove flannel numerals as the cars have problems. Who will help car 7?

 ## Concepts of Print

pages 20–21

Match spoken words to print; Match words

- Use what you know about letter sounds to find *big.* Now find *hit.* Frame and read *the.* Who can find its match? Repeat with *to.*

Extra Support/ Intervention

Discuss any words that may have caused confusion during the first reading: *banners, ignition, rev, rubber, muffler,* and *swerve.*

COMPREHENSION SKILL
Making Predictions

page 24

• Look at the flannel board. Which car will be the winner?

 COMPREHENSION STRATEGY
Question

page 30

Review the questions posed before reading to see if they were answered.

Responding

Oral Language: Retelling Children can take turns playing announcer in a retelling of the story. Each child uses a toy microphone to provide commentary for one or two pages and then passes the microphone to the next announcer.

Practice Book Children will complete **Practice Book** page 57 during small group time.

Art Center

Materials drawing paper • crayons or markers

Review the jobs shown in the story: announcer, driver, starter, crew members, firefighters, vendor. Ask children to draw and write about some jobs they would enjoy.

I can put out fires.

I can tell you to go and stop.

Practice Book page 57

Name _____

1.   2.

THEME 7: Wheels Go Around
Week Three *Vroom, Chugga, Vroom-Vroom*
Making Predictions, Responding

Children
1. think about the troubles some of the race cars had in the story and color all the cars they think have a chance to win the race
2. draw a picture of the one car they predict will win

Home Connection
Let me tell you why I thought the car I drew would be the winner of this race. Which one do you think might win? Why?

57

OBJECTIVES

- Identify words with initial consonant *d*, /d/; *z*, /z/.
- Blend and read words with *b, d, f, g, p, r, z,* and short *i*.

Materials

- **Alphafriend Cards** *Dudley Duck, Iggy Iguana, Zelda Zebra*
- **Letter Cards** *a, b, d, f, g, i, m, N, n, p, r, S, t, z*
- **Alphafriend CD** Theme 7
- **Blending Routines Card 1**

Practice Book page 58

Name _____

┌─────────────────────┐
│   fit   dig   Zig   │
└─────────────────────┘

1. _____
   See Dan
   ☺ ☹

2. _____
   See _____ dig.
   ☺ ☹

3. _____
   Can Zig and Dan _____?
   ☺ ☹

THEME 7: Wheels Go Around
Week Three
Phonics: Short *i* Words

Children
• read the sentences and write words with short *i* to complete them
• mark the smile (yes) or the frown (no) to show whether the pictures go with the sentences

Home Connection
Let me read these sentences to you! Then will you help me write the letters *Z, i, d, h, f, g* and *r* on separate scraps of paper? Then we can see how many words we can build with them.

58

Monitoring Student Progress

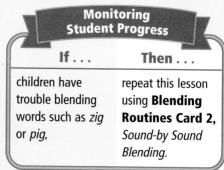

If . . .	Then . . .
children have trouble blending words such as *zig* or *pig,*	repeat this lesson using **Blending Routines Card 2,** *Sound-by Sound Blending.*

PHONICS
Blending Short *i* Words

❶ Teach: Connect Sounds to Letters

Review consonants *d* and *z*. Ask children what letter and sound they think of when they see Dudley Duck.

- Play Dudley Duck's song, and have children clap for each /d/ word. Write *D* and *d* on the board, and list words from the song. Repeat with Zelda Zebra and /z/.

Review short *i*. Remind children that they can build words with consonant letters and a vowel ("helper letter").

- Display *Iggy Iguana.* Iggy Iguana will help us build some words today. Iggy's letter is the vowel *i*, and one sound *i* stands for is /ĭ/.
- Hold up the **Letter Card** *i*. Say /ĭ/. Listen for /ĭ/ in these words: /ĭ/ *if*, /ĭ/ *inch,* /ĭ/ *in*.

Model Blending Routine 1. Now show the **Letter Cards** *d, i,* and *g*. Have children identify each letter and the sound it stands for.

- Model blending the sounds as you point to each letter with a sweeping motion. I say the sounds in order: first /d/, then /ĭ/, then /g/. I hold each sound until I say the next one, *dĭ ĭ ĭg, dig.* I've made the word *dig*. Repeat, having children blend and pronounce *dig* with you.
- Repeat this procedure with *zig*. Then display *big, fig,* and *pig* and have children blend the sounds as you point to the letters.

❷ Guided Practice

Check Understanding Display the word *rig* and ask individuals to blend the word. Then display *fit, fin,* and *pat* and have children blend the words, modeling blending as needed. Remind children to hold each sound until they say the next one, *fff ĭ ĭ ĭt*. Continue as children blend *cat, Nan, Sam*. Display the sentence *I have a pig*. Have children read it, blending the sounds in the last word. (Underlined words are from the Word Wall.)

❸ Apply

Children complete **Practice Book** page 58 at small group time.

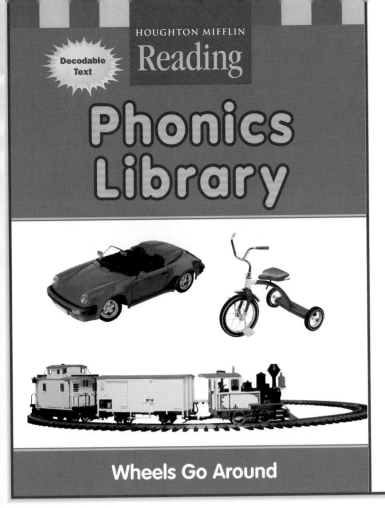

HOUGHTON MIFFLIN
Reading

Decodable Text

Phonics Library

Wheels Go Around

Zig Pig and Dan Cat
by Amy Griffin
illustrated by Amiko Hirao

15

PHONICS LIBRARY
Reading Decodable Text

Phonics/Decoding Strategy

Teacher-Student Modeling Discuss using the
Phonics/Decoding strategy to read words in the story.

Think Aloud The first word in the title begins with capital *Z*.
The sound for *Z* is /z/. I know the sounds for *i, g:*
/ĭ/, /g/. Let's blend: /z/ /ĭ/ /g/, ZZZĭĭĭg, *Zig.* Look at the first picture.
We've read about Zig and Dan before. I wonder what kind of
adventure they'll have this time.

Preview the pictures on pages 16–17. Look at the first two
pictures together. Make sure children understand that the story
takes place at the beach, where there are seashells.

OBJECTIVES

• Apply the phonics skills to decode short *i.*
• Apply high-frequency words.
• Reread for fluency practice.

Zig Pig and Dan Cat
dig for 🐚 🐚🐚 .

16

Zig Pig can dig.
I have it!

17

Prompts for Decoding

Have children read each page silently before reading with you.
Remind children to look at each letter as they sound out the
word. Prompts:

page 16 Put your finger on the word that tells what Zig and
Dan do at the beach. (dig) Have children model how they
blended *dig*.

page 17 Together, blend *Pig*. Ask: What other words here rhyme
with *Pig*? What letters are the same in those rhyming words? Zig Pig
found a shell. What do you think Dan Cat will do?

page 19 What did Zig and Dan do when they finished digging? Have
children model how they blended *sat*.

Word Key

Decodable words with short *i* ————

High-Frequency Words ————

Dan Cat can <u>dig</u>.
<u>Here</u> <u>it</u> <u>is</u>!

18

<u>Zig</u> Pig sat.
Dan Cat sat.

19

Oral Language

Discuss the story. Remind children to speak in complete sentences.

- Look at the pictures. What picture clues tell you that this story takes place at the beach? (sand, water, sunbather, digging for shells)
- Why did Zig Pig and Dan Cat dig? (They hoped to find shells.)
- What are some other things Zig Pig and Dan Cat might do at the beach? (swim, fish, run, play catch)

Use describing words. Ask children to describe the beach on a hot, sunny day. Encourage descriptions that include color, size, and weather words.

Home Connection

Children can color the pictures in the take-home version of "Zig Pig and Dan Cat." After rereading on Day 4, they can take it home to read to family members. (See **Phonics Library Blackline Masters**.)

Build Fluency

Model fluent reading.

- Read aloud page 17. Then have children read the page aloud.
- Have children reread the same page several times until each child can read it aloud smoothly.

English Language Learners

Have children say all of the lesson words aloud with you. Check for correct pronunciation of /ĭ/. Exaggerate the short vowel sound. Also help children recall the meanings of less common words such as *fig* and *rig*.

Reading Decodable Text

OBJECTIVES

- Blend consonant sounds with short *i* to read words.

Materials

- Letter Cards *a, b, d, f, g, i, n, p, q, u, r, t, z*

BUILDING WORDS
Words with Short *i*

Review building the word *dig*.

- Display **Letter Cards** *a, b, d, f, g, i, n, p, q, u, r, t,* and *z*.

- Remind children that they know all the sounds and letters to build the word *dig*. Model how to build *dig*, with **Letter Cards.** Let's stretch out the sounds: /d/ /ĭ/ /g/. How many sounds do you hear? The first sound is /d/. I'll put up a *d* to spell that. The next sound is /ĭ/. What letter should I choose for that? The last sound is /g/. What letter should I choose for that?

- Blend /d/ /ĭ/ /g/ to read d ĭ ĭ g , dig.

Model building words that rhyme with *dig*.

- Ask what letter you should change to make the rhyming word *pig*. Remove the *d* and model how to read *pig* by blending /p/ with /i/ and /g/, p ĭ ĭ g.

- Continue making and blending short *i* words by substituting *b, f, r,* and *z* for the first letter.

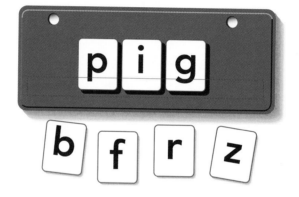

Word Wall Have a child point to the word *dig* on the Word Wall. Remind children that they can use *dig* to help them read and write words that rhyme with *dig*.

Check Understanding Have small groups work together to build short *i* words such as *pig* and *fig*. Children can use magnetic letters or other manipulative letters in your collection. Model corrections as necessary.

Extend Practice Ask children to build these words: *quit, dip, rat, ran*. Display the sentence I <u>like</u> <u>to</u> dig. Have children read it, blending the sounds in the word *dig*. (Underlined words are from the Word Wall.)

SHARED WRITING
Writing a Report

Plan a report.

- Invite children to help you write a report about some of the things they have learned about wheels during the theme.

- Together, make a graphic organizer of ideas to plan what the report will tell. Prompt children by asking questions such as: How can wheels help us? What kinds of wheels take us where we want to go? What wheels can be fun to use?

- On the chart, group children's responses into categories of main ideas about wheels.

- Have children brainstorm details to list under each main idea.

- Read through the completed chart with children. Tell them that tomorrow they will help you write a report about wheels, using the ideas on the chart.

Wheels Around Us

Wheels can help us.	Wheels can be fun.	Wheels help us go places.
police car	bike	car
fire truck	skateboard	bus
bus	skates	subway
tractor	scooter	taxi
tow truck	wagon	train

Day at a Glance
T170–T177

Learning to Read

Big Book, *T172*

Phonics: Reviewing Consonant *d* and *z*; Blending Short *i* Words, *T174*

Word Work

Building Words, *T176*

Writing & Oral Language

Interactive Writing, *T177*

Daily Routines

Sunday	Monday	Tuesday	Wednesday	Thursday	Friday	Saturday
			1	2	3	4
5	6	7	8	9	10	11
12	13	14	15	16	17	18
19	20	21	22	23	24	25
26	27	28	29	30	31	

Calendar

Reading the Calendar When children report the weather, ask if it is a good day for "cool wheels" such as skateboards, skates, or bikes. Have them tell why. Ask how weather might affect the use of other wheels.

Daily Message

Interactive Writing
Have children contribute to the daily message by telling how they have learned to use wheels. Call on children to write letters, high-frequency words, and end punctuation.

> Ken can ride a two-wheeled bike. Amy can roller-skate. Tanya races little cars.

Word Wall

High-Frequency Words Play a word game with children. I will say the alphabet, and you raise your hand when I come to a letter that begins a word on the Word Wall. *A . . .* are there any words that begin with *a?* Who will point to them and read them?

at	an	and

Word Cards for these words appear on pages R8–R10.

Daily Phonemic Awareness

Blending and Segmenting Phonemes

Read "To Market, To Market" on page 31 of *Higglety Pigglety*.

- What is this word from the poem? Put these sounds together: /j/ /ĭ/ /g/. What word is that? (jig) Continue with *hog* and *bun*.

- Next, have children count and say the separate sounds in these words: *pig, fat, jog*.

TO MARKET, TO MARKET

To market, to market, to buy a fat pig,
Home again, home again, jiggety jig.
To market, to market, to buy a fat hog,
Home again, home again, jiggety jog.
To market, to market, to buy
a plum bun,
Home again, home again,
market is done.

a Mother Goose Rhyme

31

Higglety Pigglety: A Book of Rhymes,
page 31

Getting Ready to Learn

To help children plan their day, tell them that they will—

- reread the Science Links: *Look for Wheels* and *Cool Wheels!*

- learn to build and read new words.

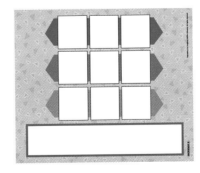

- reread the book called "Zig Pig and Dan Cat."

Zig Pig and Dan Cat
by Amy Griffin
illustrated by Amiko Hirao

15

OBJECTIVES

- Make predictions.
- Use the Summarize strategy.
- Match spoken words to print.
- Find matching words.

Big Book

Science Link

Look for Wheels

HOUGHTON MIFFLIN
Reading

AN ADAPTATION OF THE TRADITIONAL SONG
The Wheels on the Bus
Maryann Kovalski

Includes:
Science Link

Extra Support/ Intervention

Before rereading the selections, invite partners to page through the books. Children can take turns sharing what they remember about the selections, using the pictures as prompts.

INSTRUCTION

READING THE BIG BOOKS
Science Link

Building Background

Reading for Understanding Display *Look for Wheels* and read the title. Some books tell stories while others give information. Which kind of book is this? As we read this selection again, look for information about wheels.

 COMPREHENSION SKILL
Making Predictions

Student Modeling Look at the pictures on this title page. What kinds of wheels will we read about?

 COMPREHENSION STRATEGY
Summarize

Student Modeling In an information book, we look for the main idea, or what the book is mostly about. What is *Look for Wheels* about? What information can we get from this book?

 # Concepts of Print

pages 34–35

Match spoken words to print; Match words

- I will say a word from page 34. You find the word I say. Listen: *for.* Have someone point to the word. That's right. Now match the word *for* to the same word on page 35.

CRITICAL THINKING
Guiding Comprehension

pages 36–37

- **COMPARE AND CONTRAST** How are these wheels alike? How are they different?

page 38

- **MAKING JUDGMENTS** How would you answer the question on this page?

Responding

Oral Language: Summarizing Have partners choose a page to summarize for the class, telling what information they got from the words and picture.

READING THE BIG BOOKS
Science Link

OBJECTIVES
● Make predictions.
● Use the Summarize strategy.

Building Background

Rereading for Understanding Display *Cool Wheels!* and read the title. Point out that this selection also gives information about wheels.

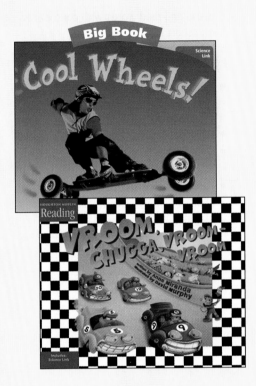

Big Book

Cool Wheels!

Science Link

Houghton Mifflin Reading

VROOM, CHUGGA, VROOM-VROOM
by Anne Miranda
pictures by David Murphy

CRITICAL THINKING
Guiding Comprehension

title page

● **MAKING JUDGMENTS** Do you think these wheels are cool? Why?

pages 36–37

● **DRAWING CONCLUSIONS** What are these men doing? (competing in races) How are they different from other bicycle and wheelchair riders?

COMPREHENSION SKILL
Making Predictions

page 39

● How do you think these children will use their cool wheels?

Responding

Literature Circle Have children tell how the selections *Look for Wheels* and *Cool Wheels!* are alike. Then have them tell how they are different.

Art Center

Materials drawing paper • crayons

Have children draw a picture of their favorite kind of wheels and add a label. Some children may be able to find an appropriate word from the selection to copy as a label.

I like my skates.

REACHING ALL LEARNERS

Challenge

Some children will be able to use language patterns from *Look for Wheels* or *Cool Wheels!* and write a new page to extend the selection. Children can draw or cut out magazine pictures of cool wheels to illustrate their work.

OBJECTIVES

- Identify initial *d* for words that begin with /d/.
- Identify initial *z* for words that begin with /z/.
- Blend and read words with consonants and short *i*.

Materials

- *From Apples to Zebras: A Book of ABC's,* pages 5, 27
- **Alphafriend Card** *Iggy Iguana*
- **Word Cards** *I, see, a*
- **Letter Cards** *a, b, c, d, f, g, i, L, n, p, r, t, v, z*
- **Picture Card** *zebra*
- **Punctuation Cards** period, question mark
- **Phonics Center** Theme 7, Week 3, Day 4
- **Blending Routines Card 1**

PHONICS
Blending Short *i* Words

From Apples to Zebras: A Book of ABC's page 5

Review consonants *d, z*. Cover the words on page 5 of *From Apples to Zebras: A Book of ABC's,* with self-stick notes. Then display the page.

- Ask children to name each picture and tell what letter they expect to see first in each word and why.
- Uncover the words so that children can check their answers.
- Repeat for the *z* words on page 27.

Review short *i*. Review with children that in order to build a word with *d* or *z* they need a vowel ("helper letter") because every word has a vowel. Ask which Alphafriend stands for the vowel sound /ĭ/.

- Display Iggy Iguana and have children name other words that start with /ĭ/. (*if, insect, itch*)

Review Blending Routine 1. Model blending the word *dig*: /d/ /ĭ//g/, dĭĭĭg, dig.

- Put **Letter Card** *f* in front of *ig*. Now let's blend my new word: /f/ /ĭ/ /g/, fffĭĭĭg, fig.
- Continue, having indivduals build and blend *big, pig,* and *rig*.

Check Understanding Display the word *zig* and ask individuals to blend the word.

For more practice, display *Liz, pit,* and *can*. Have children blend the words, modeling blending as needed. Remind children to hold each sound until they say the next one. Continue as children blend *cap, fat, tin*. Display the sentence *I like to dig*. Have children read it, blending the sounds for *dig*. (Underlined words are from the Word Wall.)

Practice/Apply Begin a sentence in a pocket chart with *I see a* and have children read it.

- For *big*, ask what letter you need to spell each sound. Then have children choose a **Picture Card** to complete the sentence.
- Repeat the activity with *Can a <Picture Card: zebra> dig?* Then have children read both sentences and blend the short *i* words.
- Have children complete **Practice Book** page 59 at small group time.
- In groups today, children will also read short *i* words as they reread the **Phonics Library** story "Zig Pig and Dan Cat." See suggestions, pages T165–T167.

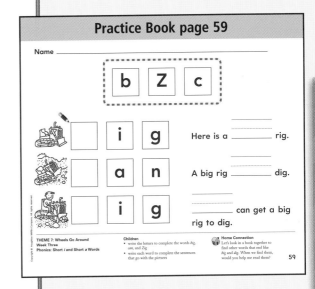

Practice Book page 59

ABC **Phonics** Center

Materials Phonics Center materials for Theme 7, Week 3, Day 4 ....

Display Day 4 Direction Chart and Workmat 5. Children build short *i* words (*big, pig, dig*) with **Letter Cards**, sound by sound. Then they use **Word** and **Picture Cards** to build the sentence *I see a big [zebra]*.

Monitoring Student Progress

If . . .	Then . . .
children have trouble building words,	have them work with you or a partner.
children can easily build and blend short *i* words,	have them build sentences using **Word** and **Picture Cards.**

Phonics **T175**

OBJECTIVES

- Blend consonant sounds with short *i* or short *a* to read words.

Materials

- **Letter Cards** *a, b, d, f, g, h, i, l, m, n, p, r, t, z*

BUILDING WORDS
Words with Short *i* or Short *a*

Review building the word *dig*.

- Display **Letter Cards** *a, b, d, f, g, h, i, l, m, n, p, r, t,* and *z*.

- Review how to build *dig* in a pocket chart. Have children listen to the word *dig*. Ask: How many sounds do you hear? The first sound is /d/. I'll put up a *d* to spell that. The next sound is /i/. I'll put up an *i* to spell that. The last sound is /g/. What letter stands for that sound? Add the letter *g* to the chart. Have children blend the word.

Review building words that rhyme with *dig*.

- Remind children that they can build words that rhyme with *dig*. What should I do to change *dig* to *fig*? Continue, using familiar consonants (*b, p, r, z*) to build other words that rhyme with *dig*.

Review building words with short *i* and short *a*.

- Repeat the activity with other short *i* words (*lit, bit, fit, pit, sit*) and short *a* words (*bat, fat, hat, mat, pat, rat, sat, fan, man, pan, ran*).

Check Understanding Have children write some short *i* and short *a* words on paper or white boards. Provide corrections as needed. Partners can exchange words and read them.

Extend Practice Have children build *fin, map, mad,* and *bag*. Exaggerate the final sound in each word to help children name the correct final consonant. Then have children read the sentence *Zig Pig and Dan Cat like to dig*. Children should recognize the underlined words from the Word Wall. Tell them to blend the other words to read the sentence.

INTERACTIVE WRITING
Writing a Report

OBJECTIVES
- Contribute to a shared report, using ideas from a graphic organizer.
- Learn academic language: *report, topic, main idea.*

Review the chart about wheels.
- Display the chart from yesterday's Shared Writing. (See page T169.)
- Review the chart with children and ask if they would like to add any more ideas. Explain that together you will use the information on it to write a report about wheels.

Wheels Around Us

Wheels can help us.	Wheels can be fun.	Whe... us.
police car fire truck	bike skateboard	ca...

Write together to tell about wheels.
- Choose a category from the chart and explain that the first part of the report will tell about that.
- Say that the first sentence should tell the reader what the main idea is. Write the heading as a topic sentence. Then have children dictate sentences for each entry listed under that main idea.
- As you write, share the pen with children. Children can supply known consonants, high-frequency words, and short *a* or short *i* words.
- On another day, add a new paragraph to the report.

Writing Center

Invite children to draw pictures to go with the report and to add captions.

This car can help us.

A bike is fun.

DAY 5
week 3

Day at a Glance
T178–T185

Learning to Read

Revisiting the Literature, *T180*

Phonics: Review Initial Consonants; Blending Short *a* or *i* Words, *T182*

Word Work

Building Words, *T184*

Writing & Oral Language

Independent Writing, *T185*

Daily Routines

Calendar

Reading the Calendar Review with children any words that were posted next to the calendar this week. Call on children to use the words in oral sentences.

Sunday	Monday	Tuesday	Wednesday	Thursday	Friday	Saturday
			1	2	3	4
5	6	7	8	9	10	11
12	13	14	15	16	17	18
19	20	21	22	23	24	25
26	27	28	29	30	31	

rainy

bus

first

last

Daily Message

Modeled Writing
After writing the message, allow each child to circle a letter they can name or box a word they can read. Children will enjoy seeing how much of the message they "know."

Today is Friday. It is Kim's turn to water the plants for the weekend.

Word Wall

High-Frequency Words Distribute cards for words on the Word Wall. Have individuals take turns using a pointer and reading a word on the Word Wall. The child with the matching word card stands and reads the card.

to   and   for

Word Cards for these words appear on pages R8–R10.

Daily Phonemic Awareness

Blending and Segmenting Phonemes

- Stack the **Picture Cards** *bug, cat, dog, goat, hen, pig, seal,* and *yak* face down. Choose a card, but don't reveal the picture.

- I'll say the sounds in this animal's name: /y//ă//k/. Raise your hand when you know what it is.

- After several cards, have children take turns being the leader, who counts the separate sounds and says them for others to blend. Add theme-related **Picture Cards** (*bike, boat, jeep, jet, van*), and give everyone a turn.

Getting Ready to Learn

To help children plan their day, tell them that they will—

- talk about books they've read in *Wheels Go Around.*

- take home a story they can read.

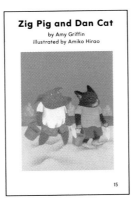

Zig Pig and Dan Cat
by Amy Griffin
illustrated by Amiko Hirao

15

- write about favorite wheels in their journals.

OBJECTIVES

- Review the week's selections.

REVISITING THE LITERATURE
Literature Discussion

Review the week's selections, using these suggestions.

- Ask what happened when Mr. Gumpy's motor car was caught in the rain.

- Have children explain the problem Grandma and the girls had in *The Wheels on the Bus.*

- Page through *Vroom, Chugga, Vroom-Vroom.* Have children tell their favorite part of the story and why.

- Take a picture walk and call on children to summarize *Look for Wheels* and *Cool Wheels!* Ask children about other special wheels they have seen.

- Have children vote for their favorite book. Read aloud the text of the winner.

COMPREHENSION SKILL
Making Predictions

Compare Books Remind children that good readers make predictions about what a book is about and what will happen next in it. Display the cover or title page of each book. Which title and book cover do you think tells best what the book is about? Why?

ON MY WAY PRACTICE READER
Dig, Zig Pig!

OBJECTIVES

- Apply phonics skills to decode short i words.
- Apply high-frequency words.
- Reread for fluency practice.

Preparing to Read

Dig, Zig, Pig!

Building Background Tell children that this story is about a character they have met before. Have them read his name. (Zig Pig) Then explain that Zig Pig drives a rig, which means equipment for a special job. Ask what this rig is used for. (digging)

Supporting the Reading

Preview the story to prepare children to read independently.

page 2: Zig Pig hopes to find something while he digs. What does the word *something* start with? Can you find that word on this page? What does Zig Pig think he might find?

page 3: Zig Pig hears a noise. What happened? (The rig hit something.)

page 4: What did Zig Pig find this time? How does he feel about that?

pages 6–7: Has Zig Pig quit digging yet? When you read this part, you will see that he does not want to quit! Find the word *not* on page 6. What do you think Zig Pig will find?

Prompting Strategies

- Try again. This page names what Zig Pig found.
- You said _____. Does that have the right sounds? Does it make sense?
- You were almost right. Read the line again and see if you can find the problem.

Responding

Build Fluency Have children take turns reading aloud their favorite parts.

Extend Ask children to draw what they would like to find in a treasure chest.

Books for Small-Group Reading

The materials listed below provide reading practice for children at different levels.

Leveled Reader

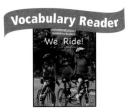

Little Big Books

Little Readers for Guided Reading

Houghton Mifflin Classroom Bookshelf

OBJECTIVES

- Build and read words with consonant sounds and short *a* or short *i*.
- Make sentences with high-frequency words.

Materials

- **Word Cards** *a, and, for, go, have, here, I, is, like, my, see, to*
- **Picture Cards** for sentence building
- **Punctuation Cards** period, question mark
- **Teacher-made word cards** *Can, big*

PHONICS
Consonants, Short *a* or Short *i* Words

① Review

Review building words with short *i* and short *a*. Tell children that they will take turns being Word Builders and Word Readers. Have a group of Word Builders stand with you at the board.

- Let's build *dig*. First, count the sounds. I know *d* stands for /d/. I also know that *i* stands for /ĭ/ and *g* stands for /g/. Let's write these letters.

- Have children copy *dig* on the board and blend the sounds.

- Now erase the *d* and add *f* in front of your letters. Children copy and ask the rest of the class (Word Readers) what new word they've made.

- Ask a new group to change places with the first one. At your direction, they erase the *f*, write *p*, and ask the Word Readers to say the new word.

- Continue until everyone builds a word by replacing one letter. Examples: *rig, zig, big; bit, pit, quit, sit; sat, pat, cat, hat, vat; van, tan, fan, man.*

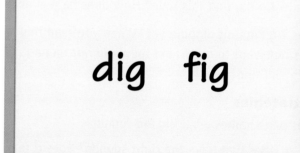

TARGET SKILL

HIGH-FREQUENCY WORDS
I, see, my, like, a, to, and, go, is, here, for, have

❷ Review

Review the high-frequency words from the Word Wall.

- Then give each small group the **Word Cards, Picture Cards,** and **Punctuation Cards** needed to make a sentence. You will need to make word cards for *Can* and *big* to build the sample sentences. Each child holds one card.

- Children stand and arrange themselves to make a sentence for others to read; as a clue, remind them that a sentence starts with a capital letter.

❸ Practice/Apply

- Children can complete **Practice Book** page 60 independently and read it to you during small group time.

- Have children take turns reading selections from the **Phonics Library** aloud to the class. Each child might read one page of "Zig Pig and Dan Cat" or a favorite **Phonics Library** selection from the previous theme. Remind readers to share the pictures.

Use questions for discussion like the following:

- Do you hear any rhyming words? What letters are the same in those words?

- Find a word that starts with the same sound as Dudley Duck's name. What is the letter? What is the sound? Find a word that starts like Zelda Zebra's name.

- This week we practiced reading the words *for* and *have* on the Word Wall. Find the words *for* and *have* in "Zig Pig and Dan Cat."

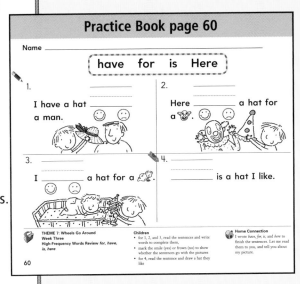

Practice Book page 60

Monitoring Student Progress

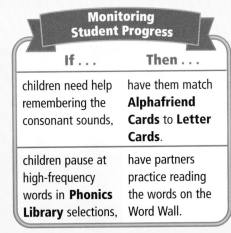

If . . .	Then . . .
children need help remembering the consonant sounds,	have them match **Alphafriend Cards** to **Letter Cards**.
children pause at high-frequency words in **Phonics Library** selections,	have partners practice reading the words on the Word Wall.

OBJECTIVES

- Blend consonant sounds with short *a* or short *i* to read words.

Materials

- **Letter Cards** *a, b, c, D, d, f, g, h, i, l, m, N, n, P, p, q, r, s, t, u, v, z*

BUILDING WORDS

Words with Short *i* or Short *a*

Build words that rhyme with *an*.

- Model how to build *an*, stretching out the sounds. Remind children to hold each sound as they say the next one, *ăăăn*.

- Along the bottom of the pocket chart, place the letters *b, c, D, f, m, N, p, r, t,* and *v.* Let's build the word *can*. What letter should I take from here to make *can*? Have a child take the letter *c*, place it in front of *an*, and model blending *can*.

- Continue building short *a* words, using initial consonants *f, m, N, p, r, t,* and *v.* On chart paper, keep a list of all the words you make, and reread the list together. Examples: *an, can, Dan, fan, man, Nan, pan, ran, tan, van, cat, mat, pat, rat.*

Build words with short *i*.

- Continue the activity with short *i* words. Examples: *it, bit, fit, hit, lit, pit, sit; dig, big, fig, pig, rig, zig.*

Check Understanding Have small groups work together to build short *a* and short *i* words with alphabet blocks or other materials. Provide corrections as necessary. Children can check the Word Bank section of their journals to see if there are other words they would like to add.

Extend Practice Have children build words using *Pam, rat, quit,* and *nap.* Exaggerate the final sound in each word to help children name the correct final consonant. Display the sentence *I see a tan van.* Have children read it, blending the sounds for *tan* and *van.* (Underlined words are from the Word Wall.)

INDEPENDENT WRITING
Journals

OBJECTIVES
● Write independently.

Materials
● journals

Preparing to Write

● Explain that today children will write sentences to tell about their favorite kind of wheels.

● Pass out the journals.

● This week we talked about the different ways people can travel, including ways to travel on the water and in the air. What new words could you put in your journal?

● We also worked together to write a report on wheels. Let's look at our charts. We had three main ideas and lots of details. Which main idea might you like to write about?

Writing Independently

● Have children draw and write about their favorite kind of wheels. Remind them that they can refer to classroom charts, the Word Wall, and the theme books as they write.

● If time permits, invite children to share what they've written with the class.

Portfolio Opportunity

Mark journal entries you would like to share with parents. Allow children to choose their best efforts or favorite works for sharing as well.

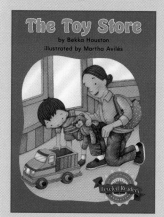

The Toy Store

Summary: *A boy walks around a toy store, carrying his teddy bear and examining all the toys that interest him. He checks out a truck, a car, a bike, a sled, and a plane. When he finds a wagon, he puts his teddy bear inside, and then looks at even more toys.*

Story Words

We *p. 2*
can *p. 2*
in *p. 2*
the *p. 2*
store *p. 2*

High-Frequency Words

Review Words

see *p. 2*
a *p. 2*

Building Background and Vocabulary

Tell children that this story is about a boy who takes his teddy bear to a toy store to look at all the toys. Preview the story illustrations and encourage children to tell about their own experiences in toy stores. Ask children to describe a special stuffed animal or toy that they like to take with them when they go out.

⚙ Comprehension Skill: Making Predictions

Read together the Strategy Focus on the book flap. Remind children to use the strategy and to stop, as they read the story, to make predictions about what the story will be about and what will happen next.

Responding

Discussing the Book Ask children to share their personal responses to the book. Begin by asking them to talk about what they liked best about the story or what picture they liked best. Ask children to talk about special toys they have seen in a toy store. Did they ever walk around a store trying lots of toys? Ask children why they think the boy has his own teddy bear with him in the store.

Responding Have children answer the questions on the inside back cover. Then help them complete the Writing and Drawing activity. Have children take turns explaining their drawing to the class and reading the label. Ask them to tell a story about where the toy in the picture came from.

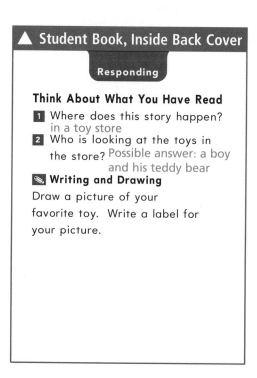

▲ **Student Book, Inside Back Cover**

Responding

Think About What You Have Read

1 Where does this story happen? in a toy store
2 Who is looking at the toys in the store? Possible answer: a boy and his teddy bear

✎ **Writing and Drawing**

Draw a picture of your favorite toy. Write a label for your picture.

Building Fluency

Model Ask children to follow along as you reread pages 2 and 3 to them. Point out that the last three words, *in the store*, on the two pages are the same. Tell children that these words appear on every page in the book.

Practice Invite children to look through the book and find the words *in the store* on every page.

Oral Language Development

Vehicle Words Discuss with children words that name vehicles. Explain that these words tell the different ways people can travel, or go for a ride. Have children page through the story to page 7, pointing to the vehicle word on each page (*truck, car, bike, sled, plane, wagon*). After they find each word on a page, have them find the vehicle in the picture. Have volunteers talk about their own experiences with the specific vehicle shown on each page.

Practice Have children practice using the vehicle words. Name a vehicle, and ask volunteers to tell about their experience with a toy or real version of that kind of vehicle.

High-Frequency Words
Review Words: *see, a*

Display the Word Cards for *see* and *a*. Read the words aloud. Ask children to listen for the words as you read page 2 in T*he Toy Store.* Ask children to say the letters in each word aloud with you. Then have them turn to page 5 in the story. Point to the Word Cards and ask children to find the words *see* and *a* in the text. Ask children to read the sentence on the page together.

see	a

Assessing Student Progress

Monitoring Student Progress

Throughout Theme 7, you monitored student progress by using the following program features: the **Emerging Literacy Survey, Guiding Comprehension** questions, **skill lesson applications,** the **Theme 7 Observation Checklist,** and the **Monitoring Student Progress** boxes.

Your students are now ready for theme assessments, which allow you to assess each student's progress formally.

Testing Options and Multiple Measures

The **Integrated Theme Test** and the **Weekly Skills Tests** are formal group assessments used to evaluate children's performance on theme objectives. Administer the **Weekly Skills Test** at the end of each week. (**Theme Skills Tests** are also available for administration at the end of each theme, beginning with Theme 2.) The **Integrated Theme Test** for Themes 7–8 can be administered at the end of Theme 8.

In addition, other multiple measures might include: the **Emerging Literacy Survey** (either using previous results or administering again at the conclusion of the theme), the **Theme 7 Observation Checklist,** and **student writing** or **artwork** (both teacher- and student-selected). Multiple measures or assessment can be collected in a portfolio.

Fluency Assessment

Oral reading fluency is a useful measure of a child's development. In the early stages, oral fluency should be observed informally. You can use the **Leveled Reading Passages Assessment Kit** to assess fluency.

Technology

Managing Assessment

The **Learner Profile CD-ROM** lets you record, manage, and report the results of children's progress.

Using Assessment to Plan Instruction

Besides the results of theme assessments, you can use the **Theme 7 Observation Checklist** on the next page to determine individual children's needs and determine how to customize instruction of major kindergarten concepts for Theme 8.

Name _____ Date _____

Observation Checklist

	Beginning	Developing	Proficient
Listening Comprehension/ Oral Language/Vocabulary • Participates in story discussions			
• Listens to a story attentively			
Phonemic Awareness • Blends phonemes			
• Segments phonemes			
Phonics • Recognizes sounds for initial consonants *d* and *z*			
• Blends and builds words with short *i*			
Concepts of Print • Uses a capital at the beginning of a sentence			
• Uses end punctuation (period, question mark, exclamation mark)			
Reading and Fluency • Reads simple decodable texts			
Vocabulary • Reads the high-frequency words *for, have*			
Comprehension • Recognizes text organization; can summarize			
• Understands cause and effect			
• Can make inferences, predictions			
Writing and Language • Writes simple phrases or sentences			
• Participates in shared and interactive writing			

Copy this form for each child. Write notes or checkmarks in the appropriate columns.
The **Observation Checklist** also appears on **Blackline Master** 100.

Resources for Theme 7

Contents

Dudley Duck's Song

(TUNE: MY BONNIE LIES OVER THE OCEAN)

Use this music for Dudley Duck's song.

Moderately   Traditional

Oh, look   at   the   dan- dy   duck, Dud- ley.

Dud- ley will   dig   all   day   long.   Dud- ley will

dive   in   the   wa- ter.   And   Dud- ley will

dance   to   this   song.

Dudley Duck's Song

(tune: My Bonnie Lies Over the Ocean)

Oh, look at the dandy
duck, Dudley.

Dudley will dig all day long.

Dudley will dive in the water.

And Dudley will dance
to this song.

Zelda Zebra's Song

(TUNE: LI'L LIZA JANE)

Use this music for Zelda Zebra's song.

Zel- da Ze- bra   likes to   zoom.   She zooms   with   zest.

Zel- da Ze- bra   zig zags   too.   She does   her   best.

Zel-   da   Ze-   bra   makes one   big   Z.

Zel-   da   Ze-   bra   zips right   past   me!

Zelda Zebra's Song

(tune: L'il Liza Jane)

Zelda Zebra likes to zoom.
   She zooms with zest.
Zelda Zebra zig zags too.
   She does her best.
Zelda Zebra makes one big Z.
Zelda Zebra zips right past me!

The Wheels on the Bus

The wheels on the bus go round and

round round and round round and

round. The wheels on the bus go round and

round all a- round the town.

The Wheels on the Bus

The wheels on the bus go
round and round
round and round
round and round

The wheels on the bus go
round and round
all around the town.

WORD LIST

In Themes 1 through 3, the Phonics Library stories are wordless stories to develop oral language. Remaining themes feature the phonics skills and high-frequency words listed here.

THEME 1
Phonics Skills:
none taught in this theme
High-Frequency Words:
none taught in this theme

Phonics Library, Week 1:
We Go to School

wordless story

Phonics Library, Week 2:
See What We Can Do

wordless story

Phonics Library, Week 3:
We Can Make It

wordless story

THEME 2
Phonics Skills:
Initial consonants *s, m, r*
High-Frequency Words: *I, see*

Phonics Library, Week 1:
My Red Boat

wordless story

Phonics Library, Week 2:
Look at Me!

wordless story

Phonics Library, Week 3:
The Parade

wordless story

THEME 3
Phonics Skills:
Initial consonants *t, b, n*
High-Frequency Words: *my, like*

Phonics Library, Week 1:
The Birthday Party

wordless story

Phonics Library, Week 2:
Baby Bear's Family

wordless story

Phonics Library, Week 3:
Cat's Surprise

wordless story

THEME 4
Phonics Skills:
Initial consonants *h, v, c;* words with short *a*
High-Frequency Words: *a, to*

Phonics Library, Week 1:
Nat at Bat

Words with short *a*: *at, bat, hat, Nat, sat*
High-Frequency Words: *my, see*

Phonics Library, Week 2:
A Vat

Words with short *a*: *hat, mat, rat, vat*
High-Frequency Word: *a*

Phonics Library, Week 3:
Cat Sat

Words with short *a*: *bat, cat, hat, mat, sat*
High-Frequency Words: *my, see*

THEME 5
Phonics Skills:
Initial consonants *p, g, f;* words with short *a*
High-Frequency Words: *and, go*

Phonics Library, Week 1:
Nat, Pat, and Nan

Words with short *a*: *Nan, ran, Nat, Pat, sat*
High-Frequency Words: *and, see*

Phonics Library, Week 2:
Go, Cat!

Words with short *a*: *Nan, ran, Van, Cat, Pat, sat*
High-Frequency Word: *go*

Phonics Library, Week 3:
Pat and Nan

Words with short *a*: *fan, Nan, ran, Pat, sat*
High-Frequency Words: *a, and, go*

THEME 6
Phonics Skills:
Initial consonants *l, k, q;* words with short *i*
High-Frequency Words: *is, here*

Phonics Library, Week 1:
Can It Fit?

Words with short *i*: *fit, it, sit*
Words with short *a*: *can, man, van*
High-Frequency Words: *a, go, I, is, my*

Phonics Library, Week 2:
Kit

Words with short *i*: *bit, fit, it, Kit, lit, sit*
Words with short *a*: *can, pan, hat*
High-Frequency Words: *a, here, I*

Phonics Library, Week 3:
Fan

Words with short *i*: *bit, quit*
Words with short *a*: *an, Fan, sat*
High-Frequency Words: *a, here, is*

THEME 7
Phonics Skills:
Initial consonants *d, z;* words with short *i*
High-Frequency Words: *for, have*

Phonics Library, Week 1:
Big Rig

Words with short *i*: *Big, dig, Rig, pit*
Words with short *a*: *can, Dan*
High-Frequency Words: *a, for*

Phonics Library, Week 2:

Can Van

Words with short *i*: *Pig, Zig, it*

Words with short *a*: *can, Dan, ran, tan, van, Cat, sat*

High-Frequency Words: *a, have, I, is*

Phonics Library, Week 3:

Zig Pig and Dan Cat

Words with short *i*: *dig, Pig, Zig, it*

Words with short *a*: *can, Dan, Cat, sat*

High-Frequency Words: *and, for, have, here, I, is*

THEME 8

Phonics Skills:
Consonant *x*; words with short *o*

High-Frequency Words: *said, the*

Phonics Library, Week 1:

Dot Got a Big Pot

Words with short *o*: *Dot, got, hot, lot, pot*

Words with short *i*: *big, it*

Words with short *a*: *Nan, Nat, sat*

High-Frequency Words: *a, and, I, is, like, said*

Phonics Library, Week 2:

The Big, Big Box

Words with short *o*: *box, Fox, not*

Words with short *i*: *big, bit, fit, hit, it*

Words with short *a*: *can, Dan, Fan, Cat, hat, mat, sat*

High-Frequency Words: *a, is, my, said, the*

Phonics Library, Week 3:

A Pot for Dan Cat

Words with short *o*: *pot, Fox*

Words with short *i*: *big, fit*

Words with short *a*: *can, Dan, Fan, ran, Cat, sat*

High-Frequency Words: *a, and, for, I, see, said*

THEME 9

Phonics Skills:
Initial consonants *w, y*; words with short *e*

High-Frequency Words: *play, she*

Phonics Library, Week 1:

Get Set! Play!

Words with short *e*: *get, set, wet*

Words with short *o*: *got, not, Fox*

Words with short *i*: *Pig*

Words with short *a*: *can*

High-Frequency Words: *a, I, play, said*

Phonics Library, Week 2:

Ben

Words with short *e*: *Ben, Hen, men, ten, get, net, pet, vet, yet*

Words with short *o*: *got, not, box, Fox*

Words with short *i*: *it*

Words with short *a*: *can*

High-Frequency Words: *a, I, my, play, said, the*

Phonics Library, Week 3:

Pig Can Get Wet

Words with short *e*: *get, wet*

Words with short *o*: *got, not*

Words with short *i*: *big, Pig, wig, sit*

Words with short *a*: *can, Cat, sat*

High-Frequency Words: *a, my, play, said, she*

THEME 10

Phonics Skills:
Initial consonant *j*; words with short *u*

High-Frequency Words: *are, he*

Phonics Library, Week 1:

Ken and Jen

Words with short *u*: *dug*

Words with short *e*: *Ken, Jen, wet*

Words with short *o*: *hot*

Words with short *i*: *big, dig, it, pit*

High-Frequency Words: *a, and, are, is*

Phonics Library, Week 2:

It Can Fit

Words with short *u*: *but, nut, jug, lug, rug*

Words with short *o*: *box, not*

Words with short *i*: *big, fit, it*

Words with short *a*: *can, tan, van, fat, hat*

High-Frequency Words: *a, he, see, she*

Phonics Library, Week 3:

The Bug Hut

Words with short *u*: *but, Bug, hug, lug, hut*

Words with short *o*: *box, Dot, got, not*

Words with short *i*: *Big, jig*

Words with short *a*: *can, Jan, fat, hat*

High-Frequency Words: *a, here, is, she, the*

Cumulative Word List

By the end of Theme 10, children will have been taught the skills necessary to read the following words.

Words with short a

at, bat, cat, fat, hat, mat, Nat, Pat, rat, sat, vat, an, ban, can, Dan, fan, Jan, man, Nan, pan, ran, tan, van

Words with short i

bit, fit, hit, it, kit, lit, pit, quit, sit, wit, big, dig, fig, jig, pig, rig, wig, zig

Words with short o

cot, dot, got, hot, jot, lot, not, pot, rot, tot, box, fox, ox

Words with short e

bet, get, jet, let, met, net, pet, set, vet, wet, yet, Ben, den, hen, Jen, Ken, men, pen, ten

Words with short u

bug, dug, hug, jug, lug, mug, rug, tug, but, cut, hut, jut, nut, rut

High-Frequency Words

a, and, are, for, go, have, he, here, I, is, like, my, play, said, see, she, the, to

I

See

see

My

my

Like

like

Use for Theme 7, Word Wall.

A

To

And

Go

a

to

and

go

Use for Theme 7, Word Wall.

Is

Here

For

Have

is

here

for

have

Use for Theme 7, Word Wall.

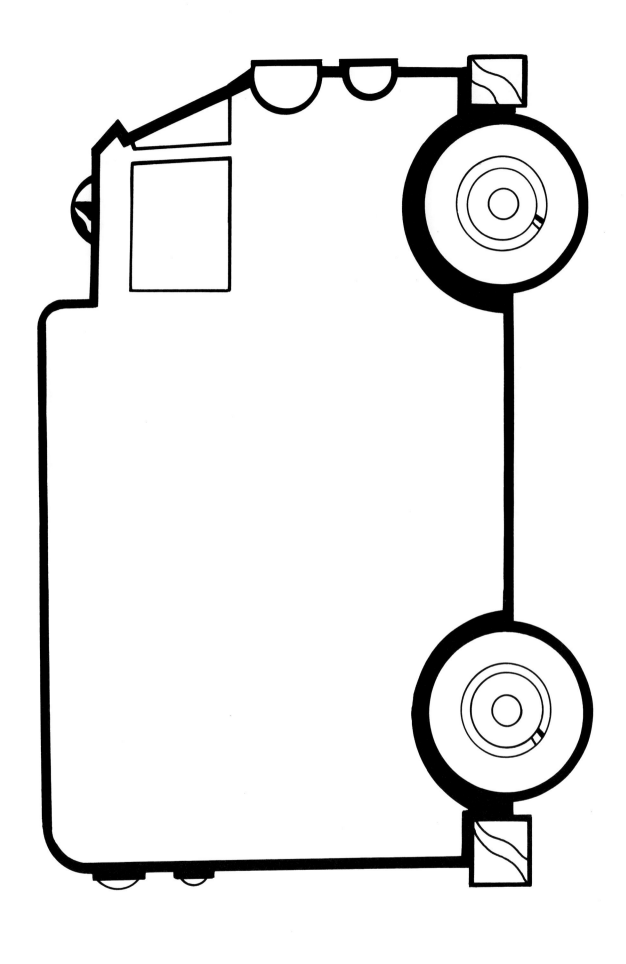

Shape Paper for The Writing Center   Use for Theme 7.

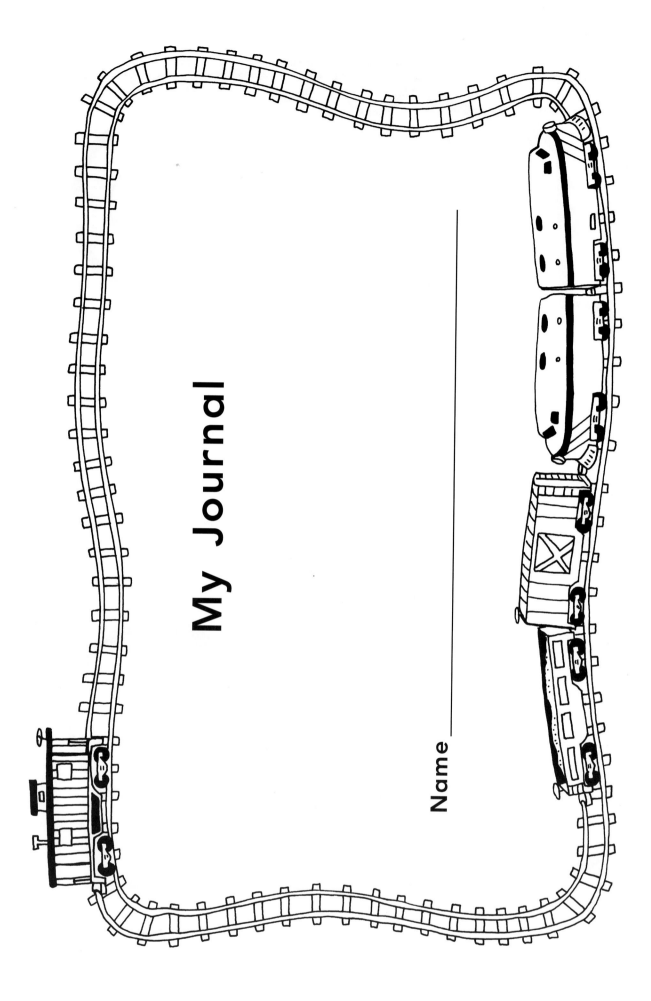

My Journal

Name _____

Use for Theme 7, Weeks 1–3, Day 5.

My Reading Log

I can read

My new words

_____   _____

- -

_____   _____

Use for Theme 7, Weeks 1–2, Day 5.

Name: _____

Good Job!

Date: _____

Use for Theme 7, Wrap-Up.

TECHNOLOGY RESOURCES

American Melody
P. O. Box 270
Guilford, CT 06437
800-220-5557
www.americanmelody.com

Audio Bookshelf
174 Prescott Hill Road
Northport, ME 04849
800-234-1713
www.audiobookshelf.com

Baker & Taylor
100 Business Center Drive
Pittsburgh, PA 15205
800-775-2600
www.btal.com

BDD Audio/Random House
400 Hohn Road
Westminster, MD 21157
800-733-3000

Big Kids Productions
1606 Dywer Avenue
Austin, TX 78704
800-477-7811
www.bigkidsvideo.com

Books on Tape
P.O. Box 25122
Santa Ana, CA 92799
www.booksontape.com
800-541-5525

Broderbund Company
1 Martha's Way
Hiawatha, IA 52233
800-716-8506
www.broderbund.com

Filmic Archives
The Cinema Center
Botsford, CT 06404
800-366-1920
www.filmicarchives.com

Great White Dog Picture Company
10 Toon Lane
Lee, NH 03824
800-397-7641
www.greatwhitedog.com

HarperAudio
10 E. 53rd Street
New York, NY 10022
800-242-7737
www.harperaudio.com

Houghton Mifflin Company
222 Berkeley Street
Boston, MA 02116
800-225-3362

Informed Democracy
P.O. Box 67
Santa Cruz, CA 95063
800-827-0949

JEF Films
143 Hickory Hill Circle
Osterville, MA 02655
508-428-7198

Kimbo Educational
P. O. Box 477
Long Branch, NJ 07740
800-631-2187
www.kimboed.com

Library Video Co.
P. O. Box 580
Wynnewood, PA 19096
800-843-3620
wwww.libraryvideo.com

Listening Library
P.O. Box 25122
Santa Ana, CA 92799
800-541-5525
www.listeninglibrary.com

Live Oak Media
P. O. Box 652
Pine Plains, NY 12567
800-788-1121
www.liveoakmedia.com

Media Basics
Lighthouse Square
P.O. Box 449
Guilford, CT 06437
800-542-2505
www.mediabasicsvideo.com

Microsoft Corp.
One Microsoft Way
Redmond, WA 98052
800-426-9400
www.microsoft.com

National Geographic School Publishing
P.O. Box 10597
Des Moines, IA 50340
800-368-2728
www.nationalgeographic.com

New Kid Home Video
P.O. Box 10443
Beverly Hills, CA 90213
800-309-2392
www.NewKidhomevideo.com

Puffin Books
345 Hudson Street
New York, NY 10014
800-233-7364

Rainbow Educational Media
4540 Preslyn Drive
Raleigh, NC 27616
800-331-4047
www.rainbowedumedia.com

Recorded Books
270 Skipjack Road
Prince Frederick, MD 20678
800-638-1304
www.recordedbooks.com

Sony Wonder
Dist. by Professional Media Service
19122 S. Vermont Avenue
Gardena, CA 90248
800-223-7672
www.sonywonder.com

Spoken Arts
195 South White Rock Road
Holmes, NY 12531
800-326-4090
www.spokenartsmedia.com

SRA Media
220 E. Danieldale Road
DeSoto, TX 75115
800-843-8855
www.sra4kids.com

Sunburst Technology
1550 Executive Drive
Elgin, IL, 60123
800-321-7511
www.sunburst.com

SVE & Churchill Media
6677 North Northwest Highway
Chicago, IL 60631
800-829-1900
www.svemedia.com

Tom Snyder Productions
80 Coolidge Hill Road
Watertown, MA 02472
800-342-0236
www.tomsnyder.com

Troll Communications
100 Corporate Drive
Mahwah, NJ 07430
800-526-5289
www.troll.com

Weston Woods
143 Main Street
Norwalk, CT 06851-1318
800-243-5020
www.scholastic.com/westonwoods

Index

Boldface page references indicate formal strategy and skill instruction.

Science activities. *See* Cross-curricular links.

Sentence building, T38, T40, **T96,** T98, **T156,** T158

Sequence of events, noting. *See* Comprehension skills.

Shared writing, T55, T115, T169

Sight words. *See* High-frequency words.

Social studies. *See* Cross-Curricular links, Reading in Science and Social Studies Center Activities.

Sounding out words. *See* Phonemic awareness, blending.

Sound-spelling patterns. *See* Phonics.

Speaking activities
   chants, rhymes, riddles, raps, **T28, T36,** T38, T56, T64, **T86, T96, T110, T146, T156, T164**
   retelling. *See* Retelling.
   sharing, T32, T42, T177, T185
   singing, T28, T34, T36, T50, T66, T86, T94, T146, T154, T164, R2–R4
   summary. *See* Summarizing, oral summaries.
   weather reports, T32, T160, T170
   See also Reading modes; Rereading.

Storytelling. *See* Retelling.

Strategic reading. *See* Strategies, reading.

Strategies, reading
   Monitor/Clarify, **T82, T92, T103, T104, T106, T118**
   Phonics/Decoding, **T51, T111, T165**
   Question, **T142, T152, T153, T162, T163**
   Summarize, **T34, T45, T48, T58, T172**

Summarizing
   oral summaries, T54, T83, T119, T143

Teaching across the curriculum. *See* Cross-curricular links.

Teaching and management
   instructional routines, T9
   management routines, T8
   Managing Flexible Groups, T20–T21, T76–T77, T136–T137
   setting up centers, T22–T23, T78–T79, T138–T139
   special needs of students, meeting. *See* Reaching All Learners.

Technology resources, R16

Text organization and structure. *See* Comprehension skills.

Theme
   Wheels Go Around, T2–T187

Theme Assessment Wrap-Up, T186–T187

Theme Poem
   "Stop and Go," T15

Theme poster, T14

Theme projects, T10–T11

Theme Skills Overview, T6–T7

Theme, Launching the, T14–T15

Think Aloud. *See* Modeling, teacher.

Viewing activities
   signs, T55

Vocabulary, extending
   antonyms, T41, T55, T56, **T149**
   color, T167
   days of the week, T42
   positional words, T89, **T99**
   size, T167
   travel words, **T159**
   weather words, T167
   See also Language concepts and skills.
   See also Building Vocabulary Center Activities; Reading in Science and Social Studies Center Activities.

Vocabulary Readers
   Let's Go!, T99
   Trolley Ride, T41
   We Ride!, T159

Vocabulary, selection
   high-frequency words. *See* High-frequency words.

Word analysis. *See* Vocabulary, extending.

Word building, T54, T62, T68, T70, T114, T122, T128, T130, T168, T176, T184

Word Wall, T30, T32, T38, T42, T52, T56, T64, T69, T80, T90, T96, T100, T114, T116, T124, T140, T150, T156, T160, T168, T170, T178, T183

Writer's craft
   opposites, T31, T41, T71, T149
   words for travel, T159

Writer's log. *See* Journal.

Writing activities and types
   cooperative writing. *See* Shared writing.
   daily message. T32, T42, T56, T64, T80, T90, T100, T116, T124, T140, T150, T160, T170, T178
   illustrate other's writing, T98, T148, T158, T185
   independent. *See* Independent writing.
   interactive. *See* Interactive writing.
   report, T169, T177
   sentences, T30, T40, T52, T88, T98, T148
   signs, T54, T63

Writing skills
   beginning, middle, end of story, **T115, T123, T131**
   formats. *See* Writing activities and types.
   main idea and details in a report, **T169, T177**
   position words, using, **T89, T99**
   prewriting skills
     observing, T55